THE FIRE OF GOD'S PRESENCE

THE FIRE OF GOD'S PRESENCE

DRAWING NEAR TO A HOLY GOD

A.W. TOZER

BETHANYHOUSE

a division of Baker Publishing Group
Minneapolis, Minnesota

Published by Bethany House Publishers
11400 Hampshire Avenue South
Bloomington, Minnesota 55438
www.bethanyhouse.com

Bethany House Publishers is a division of
Baker Publishing Group, Grand Rapids, Michigan

Printed in the United States of America

ISBN 978-0-7642-3402-6

Cover design by Rob Williams, InsideOutCreativeArts

James L. Snyder is represented by The Steve Laube Agency.

24 25 26   7 6 5 4

CONTENTS

Contents

INTRODUCTION

No theme was more important to Dr. A.W. Tozer than the presence of God, especially the manifest, tangible presence of God. It dominated Dr. Tozer's ministry and his life. Indeed, a friend of his shared with me a story that emphasizes this.

Tozer was the speaker at a summer camp meeting. He often preached at camp meetings all over the country. In his day he was quite a popular speaker at camps, colleges, and churches.

During this particular camp, Dr. Tozer was scheduled to preach at the seven o'clock evening service. When the time arrived, he was nowhere to be found. They started the service, thinking perhaps he was running late and would come in the middle, in time for his speaking.

Time went by, but Tozer never showed up, and somebody else stepped in at the last minute to preach.

The next morning my friend ran into Dr. Tozer and asked, "Where were you last night? We were waiting for you to speak."

Looking at him, Tozer quietly said, "I had a more important appointment last night."

Later on, my friend found out what had really happened. After lunch, Dr. Tozer had gone to his knees to pray and to worship God. He got lost in the presence of God and lost all sense of time.

A big concern of Tozer's was that although most churches he was familiar with believed in the presence of God, few *experienced* the presence of God. That makes a big difference. To experience the manifest presence of God is something that cannot be matched by anybody or anything.

One of Dr. Tozer's favorite biblical events was Moses coming before the burning bush. Tozer had a tremendous fascination with what Moses experienced there. He also believed what Moses experienced there on that mountain is possible for us today. Of course, not in the same manner. But we can experience the same God Moses experienced.

To Tozer, one of the great effects of experiencing the presence of God is the drastic separation of the believer from the world. Tozer fervently warned against allowing the culture to come into the church. Consider the story of Shadrach, Meshach, and Abed-Nego and the fiery furnace. King Nebuchadnezzar was okay with them worshiping Jehovah as long as they worshiped the king and his idol. *What harm could that be?*

This is what we're hearing today, that we need to bring the world into the church so that we can "win" the world to Christ. Yet Tozer would argue that's not what Scripture says. The church is to go out into the world and proclaim the gospel of Jesus Christ.

Experiencing the manifest presence of God equips us to go into the world and evangelize. It also equips us to separate ourselves from the world and worship God the way He desires to be worshiped.

One thing Tozer emphasizes is the fact that we cannot determine how we worship God. There are no options for us in this regard. We should worship God on His terms or not worship God at all.

Once we have discovered God and experienced Him, nothing else really satisfies us. That's a good thing.

Let this book lead you up to the mount where the burning bush is to experience God in His fullness.

Dr. James L. Snyder

CHAPTER **1**

Moses at the Burning Bush

Then Moses said, "I will now turn aside and see
this great sight, why the bush does not burn."
—EXODUS 3:3

*O gracious, heavenly Father, coming into Your presence is the
great joy of my life. It is in Your presence, O Father, that I
really discover who I am in Your eyes and what You think of me.
Amen.*

A Sunday school teacher was teaching a lesson on Moses at the burning bush. She explained to the class, "You know, Moses was a great scientist. He was a very observant man. When he saw the fire burning in the bush, his scientific spirit came out and he said, 'I'll go and examine this.'"

Nothing could be more wrong than the teacher's retelling of the story. Moses did initially wonder why the fire wasn't consuming the bush, but in this book, I am not going to refer to philosophy or psychology in trying to understand what happened to Moses at the burning bush. It cannot be understood, let alone explained, from any human point of view.

Everything in this book will center on theology. What I mean by *theology* is simply *theo* meaning "God" and *ology* meaning "the study of." Thus, I am referring to the study of God. I want to study God in the environment He wants me to study Him. I will not seek to convey my understanding, which is only human. I want you to experience the fire of God's presence. It will not be in the same way Moses did, but you and I can experience the manifest presence of God.

Apart from the Lord Jesus Christ, I would say that Moses is the best-known person in the Bible and in church history. Nobody carries the credentials that Moses had.

What we will explore in this book is how Moses discovered his identity at the burning bush and how it affected his life.

I am sure fires were not a rare sight in the mountains. What was it about this bush that brought Moses to his knees and let him discover not only God but his own identity?

When Moses approached the burning bush, he was eighty years old (Acts 7). If you remember his story, his first forty years were spent in Egypt, where he eventually rose to the top ruling level. He had quite a future in Egypt. Perhaps he would have replaced Pharaoh. But when Moses was forty, he fled to the mountains after killing an Egyptian who had attacked a Hebrew slave.

Looking at this story, I cannot imagine how confused Moses might have been. He thought he could help his people, the Israelites. He failed in that endeavor, which is why he ran away to hide, thinking his life was really over. But it was in that hiding that Moses found his identity.

I have noticed many times in my own life that God allows me to go in a certain direction that I am not fond of because He has a higher intent in mind for me. God could not do to Moses what was needed to be done while he was still in Egypt. It took forty years in the mountains for God to clean Moses from Egypt's influence and prepare him for what lay ahead.

It would be nice to sit down with Moses one night in the mountains and talk with him. After a few years, perhaps memories of Egypt had begun to fade. I can imagine, however, that as he sat outside on those starlit nights, he was beginning to think he had no real purpose in life.

How many times have we come to that point of discouragement? We try our best, but nothing works. We believe we have come to the end of ourselves and have no more purpose in life. At the right time and in the right place, though, God will open up a door that was not noticed before. I refer to this as a transforming experience.

Those first eighty years of Moses' life prepared and led him to the burning-bush experience that would not only change his life but all of history.

Moses was a good man in many respects. I believe his life to that point mirrors the majority of Christianity today. We try to do something to please the Lord, and much of what we do ends up in failure. Then comes a long dry period when we think nothing is happening and God cannot use us. We think we are at that retirement stage in life.

No doubt, we are good people and try to do good things. Just as Moses had a passion to serve his people, Christians today have a similar passion to serve. We see it all around. Moses' problem was that he did not know God and he did not know how God wanted him to serve. That is the key issue here. It is not enough to do good things. Anybody can do good things, including non-Christians and atheists, for that matter.

It is not what you are doing, but who is working through you that really makes the difference.

At the burning bush, Moses experienced transformation, and for the first time in his life he discovered his true identity. Those first eighty years were past and served only as a preparation for what was going to happen next.

That is exactly what Christians today need to experience: to come in front of that burning bush and discover their identity from God's perspective.

Everyone has dreams of what they want to do, but our dreams are based only on our limited perspective. How would our lives change if we had an eternal perspective? How would our lives change if we saw ourselves through God's eyes?

For forty years, Moses stumbled around in the mountains taking care of sheep. I cannot imagine how bored he was. After all, he was a man schooled in all that Egypt's education had to offer at the time. Yet here he is, seemingly doing nothing of real significance year after year, decade after decade. Think of it, if Moses had died at age seventy-nine, nobody would ever have heard of him or known of him today.

What interests me about Moses' story is, God's timing is never my timing and God's place of encounter is never one I would pick. Moses had to submit himself to God in all respects. He had to give up everything and even walk away from his people. This commitment led God to bring Moses to the burning bush.

Who would pick an eighty-year-old man and send him to do the task Moses was sent to do? Our thinking today is that we need young people with energy to do that. However, God's plan seldom coincides with our plans. God's ideas are far above our ideas because we are limited by our human thinking.

When God calls a person to do a work, that person has access to the authority and unlimited resources of God.

After Moses left Egypt, he joined a family in the mountains, married a daughter of that family, and probably thought his life had been settled. The end. What Moses did not know was God was watching him. He did not know how much his life was going to change after seeing the burning bush.

What I hope to accomplish in this book is to better understand Moses' experience at the burning bush. As I said earlier, not to understand it from an educational or philosophical point of view, but rather from a theological point. I want to try to understand what Moses experienced, how it changed and transformed his life, and how you and I can experience the fire of God's presence, too. If we are truly going to be used of God today, we need to embrace our own burning-bush experience.

All Creatures of Our God and King

Thou flowing water, pure and clear,
Make music for thy Lord to hear.
Alleluia! Alleluia!
Thou fire so masterful and bright,
Thou givest man both warmth and light!
O praise Him, O praise Him!
Alleluia! Alleluia! Alleluia!

—St. Francis of Assisi (1181/82–1226) /
William H. Draper (1855–1933)

CHAPTER 2

The Foundation for Experiencing the Presence of God

Now this is the main point of the things we are saying: We have such a High Priest, who is seated at the right hand of the throne of the Majesty in the heavens.

—HEBREWS 8:1

Almighty God, my heart yearns so much for You, and to experience Your presence. Your words in my heart today will be the platform of my obedience. In Jesus' name, amen.

A delight of my Christian experience through the years has been what I call coming into the presence of God. Nothing makes my day more blessed than knowing He is not only in me, but I am also in Him.

To learn what it means to be in the presence of God, we need to understand the dynamics of His presence. The book of Hebrews gives us a picture of a high priest seated on the right hand of the throne "of the Majesty in the heavens" (8:1). What is this "Majesty in the heavens" all about? And how do we ready ourselves to experience the burning bush?

The first step is to focus our attention on God himself— what kind of God He was, is, and will ever be. I can do little more than say this is fundamental to our Christian faith: believing that God—the Majesty—is in the heavens. This is also fundamental to human sanity. If we rule God out of our thinking and out of the universe, then we are curious and wonderful relics of what? Nobody knows. If we rule God out of our thinking and out of the universe, we simply have deep longings for what is not and has never been.

This idea that God exists and is the sovereign Majesty in the heavens is also fundamental to human morality. A wide difference exists between the person who fears God and the person who doubts His existence or does not believe at all. Believing we are from God gives us an upward moral trust we could not possibly have otherwise. The expectation of reporting to God any sinful deeds done in the body is a strong power to hold our souls together.

As believers, we must fear God and know He will bring every work into judgment, whether good or evil. No adequate view of human nature is possible until we believe that we came from God and should go back to God again. We must have faith in God, the rock on which we build.

Tradition has it that Saint Patrick recited this prayer every day:

> I arise today through a mighty strength, the
>   invocation of the Trinity,
> through a belief in the Threeness,
> through confession of the Oneness
> of the Creator of creation.

Indeed, when we rise in the morning, it ought to be in almighty strength and belief in God the Father Almighty, maker of heaven and earth.

The Bible teaches that creation is a universe—all we see around us, from the farthest star spotted by the most powerful telescope, down to the tiniest cell seen through a microscope. And everything in this vast single system is united and works harmoniously.

If everything in the world were independent of everything else, we would have a cancer throughout the vast universe. But God brings everything together and interlocks them, making them interdependent, not independent.

The Bible further teaches that this great interlocking system, this universe (*uni* meaning "one"), has a central control. That central control is called the throne of God; it is controlled from that center.

It seems logical that if an organism, such as the human body, had no center or central control, it would absolutely be dysfunctional. Every organization must have a head or else there can be no harmony, no coordination, no cooperation, and no life.

Everything organized must have a head, starting with the simplest group. The president of a group must preside if only half a dozen is present. The same is true right on up to the largest empire in the world.

From this central control, the throne of God, God governs His universe according to an eternal purpose. His eternal purpose embraces all things. Those two little words—"all things"—appear often in the Scriptures. *All things* are bigger than the sky above and all the worlds they take in. Therefore, we have the Majesty in the heavens, sitting upon His throne, as well as someone at His right hand.

Who is He? He is Jesus Christ, the minister of the sanctuary, which God, not man, made. The reason for His being there? In all this interdependent, interrelated, and interlocking universe, one province revolted and said, "We don't want to be ruled by the head. We will not be ruled from the throne. We will rule ourselves and build this great Babylon up to heaven. We will not have God ruling over us." That province, which we call humankind, inhabits the little rolling sphere: earth.

With one sweep of His hand, God could have knocked that province out of existence, but what did He do? God sent

His only begotten Son to redeem that province and bring it back into the sphere of the throne again.

No sinner recognizes the throne of God as being valid. He rejects the right of God to rule over him. He may talk about God, appeal to God, use the name of God, but he will not obey God. But when a sinner repents and is born again, he leaves the old world—the old province that revolted—and moves into the kingdom of God and under His rule. That is how simple it all is.

You cannot come into the kingdom by being baptized, although we all ought to be baptized according to the teaching of Jesus. We do not get there by joining churches, though we all ought to join a church. And you do not get there by praying; you can pray to the end of your life, twenty-four hours a day, and not get there. It is Jesus Christ the Lord who gets you out of the old revolted province and into the kingdom of God, under the rule of the throne of God again.

God became man to rescue us, and then Christ Jesus forfeited His own life to bring back to God those who had revolted.

God's message is that we have Somebody sitting on the throne who was one of us. That message thrilled the early church. If those early men and women who were baptized by the Holy Ghost (Acts 2) were here, we would never hear them talking about the political and industrial questions exciting ministers today. They talked about God, the throne and Christ at the Father's right hand, the coming again of Jesus and the consummation of all things, the downfall of iniquity and the purification of the world, and the cleansing of the heavens above.

Those new Christians in the early church surely proclaimed everywhere: "Did you know that one of us is in a position equal to God, next to God in power and authority, and with all power given unto Him in heaven and earth?"

The person who is joined to God is victorious. Therefore, if we are in Him, we too can be victorious. Christians ought to recognize their nature has been joined to God's nature by the mystery of the incarnation. When Christ died on the cross, rose again, and began to join individual Christians to His body, He meant that we were to have the same victory and high privilege He has at God's right hand.

Jesus did everything to make unbelieving people see that they have the same place in the heart of God that Jesus himself has. Not because we are worthy of it, but because He is worthy of it and He is our head. Christ Jesus is the victorious man, the representative man before God, the model man, after which we are patterned. That is why the Lord will not let us alone.

I recommend we raise our eyes to God, the Majesty in the heavens, that we look hard and reverently and see at God's right hand one of us. May we all say, "If Christ Jesus is there, I can be there. If He is accepted of God, I am accepted in Him. If God loves Him, He loves me. If He is safe, I am safe. If He has conquered, I can conquer. And if He is victorious, I can be victorious."

Let us seek the face of God in Jesus Christ, always remembering, "No one comes to the Father except through Me" (John 14:6). So, let us come and practice it. Let us move into the heart of God and live there victoriously.

Come, Holy Ghost, Our Hearts Inspire

Come, Holy Ghost, our hearts inspire;
Let us Thine influence prove:
Source of the old prophetic fire,
Fountain of life and love.

—Charles Wesley (1707–1788)

CHAPTER 3

Made for His Presence

Where can I go from Your Spirit? Or where can I
flee from Your presence?

—PSALM 139:7

*No matter my situation, O God, You are there. Your presence is
the identifying factor of who I am. I praise You for my identity
in You. Praise You, O God, in Jesus' name, amen.*

The basic truth I am pursuing is that God made us so that we might know Him, live with Him, and enjoy Him. The human race has been guilty of revolt. Men and women have broken with God. The Bible says we are alienated from God and strangers to Him. We have ceased to love Him and trust Him and, most important of all, ceased to enjoy His presence.

As David expressed, the Lord is everywhere.

> Where can I go from Your Spirit? Or where can I flee from Your presence? If I ascend into heaven, You are there; if I make my bed in hell, behold, You are there. If I take the wings of the morning, and dwell in the uttermost parts of the sea, even there Your hand shall lead me, and Your right hand shall hold me.
>
> —Psalm 139:7–10

No one can escape God's presence. But experiencing the up-close manifest presence of God is something else. And this is the presence of God that we are to enjoy. That is what Moses discovered at the burning bush.

It is not enough to live by faith if we mean "faith" without any manifestation on God's part. Since I am a personality and God is a personality, I can have an ongoing relationship with God.

It is no proof that we have great faith if we solemnly, glumly say, "I believe," and never allow God to give a response to our faith. Of course, there are times when we walk by faith and not by sight—times when God for His own goodness has hidden His face from us. As written in Isaiah 54:8: "I hid My face from you for a moment; but with everlasting kindness I will have mercy on you." Again, we must learn to live in God's manifest presence, which is the difference between revival and every other state of spirituality a church might know.

God wants to manifest himself to His people. In the Old Testament, we have a picture of this presence of God called the tabernacle. This is a reflection of the burning bush that Moses experienced. I might even say it is the fulfillment of that burning bush. Let me briefly describe the tabernacle.

The Lower Court

The Lower Court was not inside the structure; rather, it was outside and referred to as the court of the Gentiles.

I liken this Lower Court to people interested in religion but far from God, who, nevertheless, may be practicing religion. Practicing rituals of various kinds, counting their beads, unconsciously moving their lips on the bus or airplane. Or maybe they are paying respect to religion. When a baby is born or somebody is married or a christening or a funeral, they manage to get to church. These people pay token respect to religion but give no regard to God's way or God's cross or God's redemption.

The Inner Court

The next step was the inner court, where there was a laver and a great brazen altar, which was not a pretty thing at all.

It was like a topless furnace with a grate underneath where you put a fire and then on top put a beast and stirred the pot. The beast would burn up in ugly smoke.

This altar is where lambs, the beasts, the red heifer, and other creatures were brought to sacrifice.

When we sugarcoat how sacrifices were made, when we diminish the slaughterhouse element of them, we diminish what happened on the cross.

It must have been an unpleasant thing to see a man dying on a cross on the side of the hills in Jerusalem. Poets have made our Lord's death sound so beautiful that we send picture cards about it for Easter. But it was not a beautiful sight at all. There a man stripped naked hanged in the hot April sun, bleeding from His hands, feet, side, and forehead. There a man suffered and writhed, groaning from the pain of it all. Why was the man on the cross? Because there was only one thing worse than that, and that was hell itself where men were going.

God sent His only begotten Son that He might go to the cross, stop the gates of hell and shut them up so that those who believe in Him should not perish but have everlasting life. So let us not get too nice about Christ's death. It was a slaughter hill where He died. A man—God's Son—died in a terrible situation because of sin. He died in pain because sin is a painful thing. A man died, ostracized and forsaken, because sin brings ostracism and forsakenness.

The Laver

The next step in the tabernacle's inner court was the laver. When you passed the altar, you came to a great bowl, which looked like a huge punch bowl standing up there, from where people washed. The laver was sprayed with water, and everything was washed there. Beyond the laver is the altar where the lamb died, which was the inner court. This is a picture of God's plan for us today. We first must come from the cross where Christ, the Lamb of God, died, and by His blood we experience the washing of water by the Word, allowing us to go to the next step.

The Veil

Worshipers could enter where the altar and laver were, but then there was another area in the tabernacle, shut off by a huge veil, where nobody could enter except the High Priest. For unless you repent, you cannot see the kingdom.

Pieces of furniture were positioned in the holy place, including a light of seven candlesticks. Our Lord said, "I am the light of the world." When you have come by the cross and are cleansed and enlightened, the Holy Ghost says you can be enlightened. And there in the holy place, the sevenfold Spirit shined His light.

Behind the veil was also a table that held shewbread, the bread of His presence, and an altar of incense.

After Jesus fed the five thousand, He told crowds they should "labor . . . for the food which endures to everlasting life" (John 6:27).

"Our fathers ate bread," replied the Pharisees, referring to the manna God provided in the desert.

"Yes," Jesus said, "but the bread your fathers ate was only temporary bread. I have come that you might have bread, and if you eat of it you shall never die."

They said, "Give us that bread," and He replied, "I am the bread of life."

But many turned away; they could not accept His words. Too doctrinal, too strong. If there had been a preacher preaching like that they would have said, "We love our brother, but let's get rid of him. We think it's too strong to say that Jesus is the bread and we eat of Him." Nevertheless, that is what it says in figure, in type, in the Old Testament, and in blunt language in the New Testament.

The Altar of Incense

Also behind the tabernacle veil was the altar of incense. What was that burning on the altar, filling that little room with the sweet-smelling incense? It was prayer.

To me this is a beautiful picture. Christ's church ought to be a place that is lit by the light of the world shed forth by the sevenfold Holy Spirit. A place where we gather to eat of the bread of life, not only communion Sunday, but all the time, every Sunday, all while the altar of incense sends up a sweet spiral of fragrant perfume—sweet to God and pleasing in His nostrils. Add to this, the sound of prayer, pleasant in His ear, and the sight of an enlightened people gathered together, pleasant to His eyes.

The light of the world is Jesus. We Christians have not a little light; we possess the light of God. We pray that seekers around us find the light in our churches. For that church, I would give everything I have. If I knew that kind of church could be in the world now, I would not hesitate to give the blood out of my veins.

When we walk and know we are walking where the light shines—where there's bread to eat, where there's a prayer to be made that goes to the ear of God with acceptance—that is the church.

I love the church, for it is a company of people committed to this faith and this kind of belief.

The cleansing blood is here so you and I can come into the manifold presence of God. The question is, Have we done it? Are we doing it? I hope so, but to those who have not experienced God's presence, I point to the cross where He died, the blood that cleanses, the Holy Ghost who is the light, and to the living Lamb that gives the bread. I tell you that you have a right to enter God's tabernacle and be a priest of the Most High God. We have no need for a Melchizedek or Aaron. Your prayers can rise cleansed by the blood, enlightened by the Holy Ghost, into the very presence of God.

This is a short review of the tabernacle. An entire book could be devoted to the subject. What I want to do is lay down the basis of our burning-bush experience. We can come into God's presence because of what Christ did for us to enjoy our true identity in Him.

I Love Thy Kingdom, Lord

I love thy kingdom, Lord,
the house of thine abode,
the church our blest Redeemer
saved with his own precious blood.
—Timothy Dwight (1752–1817)

CHAPTER 4

The School of Silence Prepares for the Burning Bush

Be still, and know that I am God; I will be exalted
among the nations, I will be exalted in the earth!
—PSALM 46:10

*In the silence of the night, O God, I begin to understand my
relationship with You. O how wonderful You are in all aspects of
my life. Praise You, in Jesus' name, amen.*

Nobody who knows anything about Moses would question that he is a great man. At this point in the biblical narrative, however, his greatness was hidden, undeveloped, and unmanifested to him.

A great career, we might say, was about to open up before Moses. He was to be many things to many people for a long time. It might seem to be overstating the case, but it is difficult to overstate Moses. He was a prophet, and it was said that Christ was a prophet like unto Moses. He was a lawgiver. He received from God by the ministration of angels the greatest moral code ever given to mankind. There have been great moral codes given. Many familiar with Greek thought and history know Lycurgus gave to Sparta a system of laws lasting some five hundred years. Then there is the Constitution of the United States, the greatest document created by the mind of man. A great system of laws lies there, but the greatest of all was that given by God through Moses.

Moses made his fame as an emancipator, a setter free of slaves, a leader, a statesman, and a teacher of the ages. All this he was to be, and he was already well prepared.

Have you ever stopped to think that at this time in his life, Moses was so well educated he could have been a bishop in any denomination today or eagerly sought after as a pastor? This man was so great, educated in Pharaoh's court with all the wisdom of the Egyptians. He could have been a great politician.

There is something about courts where there is royalty. It is a bit different, and people who have been there and exposed to it for a while are never quite the same again. Brought up at the feet of the great Pharaoh, this man Moses was called the son of Pharaoh's daughter and sat on the knee of many potentates and kings and royal figures occupying the great land of Egypt in that day.

After running from Egypt, Moses went for a postgraduate course more beneficial than his education at the feet of the great teachers of Egypt. He went to the school of silence, and to the sheep and the stars in the heavens above. All through the evenings, before sleep overtook him, he listened to the silence and learned to know himself.

We moderns of today's civilization know everything but ourselves. We don't know ourselves because we can't get quiet enough. Fly on a plane somewhere and your ears continue to buzz for the next five hours. God took this man out of the noise and put him in the silence where he could hear his own heartbeat. That was a postgraduate course the like of which you don't get in schools today.

Later on, David understood this when he wrote, "Be still, and know that I am God" (Psalm 46:10). David discovered who he really was when he became aware of who God was. This knowledge of God must come out of the stillness and silence of our lives. We must push everything else aside and allow the silence to open up our hearts and minds.

It took Moses forty years on the mountain of silence to rid himself of Egypt. During those forty years he began to understand himself and realized God was leading and directing him. He had no aspirations of the future at this time in his life. He was doing what he thought he would be doing for the rest of his life, and that silence brought him to a place of absolutely no expectation on his part.

Moses went to the sheep for silence. The Bible does not hesitate to tell us to go to the lower animals for lessons. "Go to the ant, you sluggard! Consider her ways and be wise" (Proverbs 6:6), said the Holy Ghost through the prophet. Our Lord said, "Consider the lilies, how they grow: they neither toil nor spin; and yet I say to you, even Solomon in all his glory was not arrayed like one of these" (Luke 12:27).

And Isaiah claimed that Israel was not as wise as the ox that lived where his new crib was and came back every night to its master's crib (Isaiah 1:3).

Again, it was not uncommon for the Lord to send people to the school of low animals. But Moses, this learned man with tremendous intellectual capacity, an elite Egyptian education, and upbringing in Pharaoh's court, was not prepared for what God had in mind when he was sent to school among the sheep.

Ralph Waldo Emerson wrote in his *Nature* essay, "If a man would be alone, let him look at the stars." Moses had occasion to look at the stars all during the evening and all night long if he cared to and whenever he awoke in the night. When you want pure loneliness, absolute solitude, look at the stars; for the stars make no noise, they simply burn on in their magnificence.

Emerson also said, "If the stars should appear one night in a thousand years, how would men believe and adore; and preserve for many generations the remembrance of the city of God which had been shown! But every night come out these envoys of beauty, and light the universe with their ad-monishing smile." The reason we pay so little attention to the city of God that shines yonder is there is so much noise and so many distractions.

Still, for Moses, whatever he understood about sacred-ness from the quiet of the wilderness and being under the stars was nothing in comparison to what he discovered, kneeling before the burning bush. This underscores the importance of discovering the burning bush for ourselves. Prior to this experience, Moses was just like anybody else when it came to reverence. Sacredness and reverence are not things we can create within our own human experi-ence. Apart from this burning-bush experience, we are at great loss.

The greatest loss modern man has suffered is not the loss of limbs. The loss of the home, as tragic and terrible as that is, is not the greatest loss some of us have suffered. The loss of loyalty and the loss of law keeping; all these are losses but spring out of another loss basic to these. These are not the worst losses we could experience. The worst is losing the sense of sacredness.

I grieve when I come into the average fundamental evan-gelical gospel church. There's so little of the sense of God in it. You never bow your head with reverence unless you have deliberately disciplined yourself to do it because there is not a sense of sacredness. Anything goes, and this is a loss too terrible even to be appraised. The world has hidden God from our sight and secularism has taken over. We have secularized worship, the gospel, and even Christ. I say that it's a great and tragic loss, and no great man can come out of that kind of thing. No great movement can spring out of that kind of thing. God may have to sweep it away from us and start somewhere else.

The kind of revival we need today is a revival of reverence and sacredness in the presence of God. This needs to happen personally and then flow over into the church setting. This lack of sacredness and reverence has become a wall, keeping us from experiencing God's presence.

Worship always leads to this awesome moment of sacredness and reverence. We ought to take off our shoes, put aside everything else, and focus on the One who is revealing himself to us in that moment.

The Christian church today has lost this essence of what worship is all about. Worship is not about stirring up emotional enthusiasm. If it is true worship, it will bring a person or a group of people to a point of absolute silence and reverence in His presence. Apart from this, we are not experiencing God.

Our Sunday-morning worship should be the culmination of our worship throughout the week. If what we do Sunday morning cannot be duplicated the rest of the week, perhaps what we're doing Sunday morning is not true worship in God's sight.

Charles Finney, the great evangelist, was a preacher on fire for God, no question about that. When he felt the fire beginning to recess in his life and ministry, he stopped everything he was doing, went out into the woods, got down on his knees before God, and stayed like that until the fire returned.

My recommendation for the Christian church today is to call a moratorium on all activity and focus on coming into worship until the fire descends and engulfs us in the sacredness of His presence.

What Moses was before the fire experience was nothing compared to what he was afterward. The great man used of God was created in front of that burning-bush experience. And that fire never went out for the rest of Moses' life. The experience was absolutely a crisis for Moses.

I Will Praise Him

Then God's fire upon the altar
Of my heart was set aflame.
I shall never cease to praise Him.
Glory, glory to His name!

—Margaret Jenkins Harris
(1865–1919)

CHAPTER 5

The Fire in the Burning Bush

The Angel of the Lord appeared to him in a flame of fire from the midst of a bush. So he looked, and behold, the bush was burning with fire, but the bush was not consumed.

—EXODUS 3:2

O God, who is a consuming fire, burn deep within my heart and soul that I may know You as You are worthy to be known. Amen.

God had to give Moses a vivid, intimate personal experience of himself. Moses had to meet God in the crisis of encounter.

I am not in the habit of using words carelessly. And so, I have carefully taken the two words *crisis* and *encounter* and joined them by the little word *of*.

Our trouble comes when we are talked into the kingdom of God. We come into the kingdom of God by smooth talkers with a marked New Testament, telling us logically how we can be converted. However, they do not insist because souls do not know that there is such a thing as meeting God in the crisis of encounter, as Moses did here in a vivid personal experience.

Not that we see with our external eyes, but we see more vividly with our inner eyes. Never apologize for your inner eyes. Your inner eyes are the real eyes and your external eyes can fool you. You look out in the moonlight and see something you think is a ghost. It turns out to be a white mule or a sheep caught on a bush. Your external eyes fool you, but your inner eyes never do.

When Paul was caught up into the third heaven, he saw, but not with his external eyes. If he had seen with the eyes of the flesh, it would have burned those eyes out. For he saw with the eyes of his heart. If it is with the eyes of our heart that we encountered God with the inner man, we do not apologize for that. When this external man has turned back to dust and the wind of heaven has blown it, the internal man will still deliver him gazing upon the face of God. To be what God wanted him to be, Moses had to have an encounter with God.

How did God reveal himself to Moses?

God revealed himself as fire. God is invisible and ineffable, and He cannot tell us what He is, He can only tell us what He's like. So, He tells us that He is like fire. God is not fire, though the Scripture says our God is a consuming fire. It does not mean that physically, metaphysically, and ontologically, as the theologians would say, God is fire. The followers of Zoroaster, called Chebers or Guebers, and among the Parsees of India believe that and would get down on their knees and worship a flame of fire on an altar. But we know that God is not fire, where fire can destroy a place. Fire can bring down a building or cook a stew. God is not that kind of fire, but God is like fire.

Fire is the nearest thing to being like God that God can think of to tell His poor, half-blind children what He is like. So, God appeared here, in the twilight, with flames of fire, and Moses kneeled before Him. God spoke out of the midst of the bush, and Moses saw and felt and experienced in that encounter with God. God commissioned Moses to go out and deliver Israel, to receive the law, to organize the greatest nation in the world out of which the Messiah should come and to give His name to the ages, all because he met God.

The important thing is to understand the effect of this experience, the effect of God's presence. For remember one thing, the fire in the bush was not God. The fire in the bush was God dwelling within it and shining out through the flames. It was the presence of God, and Moses experienced God there. God was no longer merely an idea to the man. Too often God is just an idea to the average person, like He had been with Moses up to that time. Although Moses was an Orthodox Jew, he had still only perceived God in an intellectual way. Now he experienced God personally and God became an experience, not just knowledge.

Before us are at least two kinds of knowledge. There is knowledge that comes from Scripture. Then there is knowledge that comes from experience. You can describe a thing, demonstrating that you have knowledge of it, and you can give knowledge to others. However, it is another thing to experience it. You can describe the battle, but the boy going through the terror of shot and shell and gas and fire has experienced it, and the ones who experience it say very little about it.

Three of our sons went through the fire, and they talk very little about it. It is amazing—the Tozers are usually as talkative as can be—but they do not say much about that experience they went through; just a few things when they came back, never any more after that.

When you have this kind of experience, it is so vivid that you cannot escape it for a lifetime. When Moses experienced God, He was no longer history to him. God was a leading personality. The tragic breakdown in Christian circles is the substitution of doctrine for experience. We have become very good at explaining doctrine, which falls far short of experiencing this presence of God.

The Bible was never given to be an end in itself but to be a path leading us to God. When the Bible leads us to God and we have experienced God in the crisis of encounter, then the Bible has accomplished its work. It continues to work, but it has done its ultimate work. It is not enough that you should memorize the Scriptures. Some people memorize the Word of God but have never met the God who gave the Word. They can quote whole chapters, but the same Spirit that inspired the Word has never inspired them. The Bible can only be properly understood by the same Spirit that inspired it. For me to memorize whole passages of Scripture is useless, unless I go on by means of those Scriptures to meet God in the crisis of encounter.

The greatest ministry any church can have is to experience God, and then tell everybody, "I have experienced God, you too can experience God." We can know God as Moses knew the bush; we can know God as a rabbit knows the green briar patch; we can know God as a babe knows his mother's breast; we can know God for himself. If I don't do anything else in this book, I want to stir the hearts of God's people so in the end those who are borderline, who don't know where they are, will know that by the gospel, by the blood of the Lamb, by the power of atonement, by faith and this Bible and within, we can know God for himself.

My Faith Looks Up to Thee

May Thy rich grace impart
Strength to my fainting heart,
My zeal inspire.
As Thou hast died for me,
Oh may my love to Thee
Pure, warm and changeless be,
A living fire.

—Ray Palmer (1808–1887) /
Lowell Mason (1792–1872)

CHAPTER 6

Lessons from the Fire in the Bush

So when the LORD saw that he turned aside to look,
God called to him from the midst of the bush and
said, "Moses, Moses!" And he said, "Here I am."

—EXODUS 3:4

*My heart, O God, is open to You to follow by instructions,
whatever they might be. My life rests upon Your teaching, and
my commitment is unconditional obedience. Amen.*

Look at the fire in the bush and the lessons Moses got from it. I do not know that they came to him as point one, two, three, four, and five, the way some preachers teach. I only know the lessons came to him in a sudden wonderful blazing experience; fire dwelt in the bush.

The important thing here is this was not something Moses was expecting. He had spent forty years on that mountainside watching the sheep, and during that time, I am sure he saw a lot of bushes set on fire naturally. This bush, however, was an attraction to him that he could not explain.

After forty years away from Egypt, it was God's timing now to open up the next stage in Moses' life and ministry. Never does God call the equipped. Rather, He equips the called. Moses was called of God to do a work that he could never imagine. At eighty years old, Moses believed, I am sure, he was at the end of his life. The rest of his life he would be among the sheep here in the mountains.

Then Moses saw the bush and the angel next to the bush, and the fire in the bush, but the fire was not consuming the bush. Therefore, Moses had to turn aside and examine it.

The fire in the bush represents what our experience with God is all about. At the core of all this is the lordship of Jesus.

Paul calls this the mystery and hope of glory, Christ in you. Dr. A. B. Simpson preached, "Christ in you, the hope of glory" as the objective of our faith. Some churches said he was a fanatic. Some said, "It's wonderful." A new impulse came because the doctrine of dwelling in Christ was brought out and preached once more.

The acacia bush that God caused to burn was perfectly helpless in the fire. You will never know God as you should know Him until you are helpless in His hands, until you cannot escape Him. As long as you can run and go to safety, you are not in God's hands. As long as you can back out, as long as there is a bridge behind you, you can retreat. It is a poor rat that does not have at least two holes. The reason for that is no rat is ever sure of himself. He has never settled; he always wants to have a second possibility.

I find many children of God are like the burrowing rodents that farmers love to hunt. They have more than one place to hide. The farmer will get down in one hole, while the rodent will be a quarter of a mile away sitting and eating peacefully because he has more than one hole, more than one place to hide.

As Christians, we want to follow God, but we also want a second plan in case it doesn't work out.

God is the last resort for most of us. But here was a bush that could not back out of it, a plan it could not get out of there. The happy Christian caught by the Lord cannot escape because he does not want to escape and has burned all his bridges in every direction. There is no other way to go.

When Elijah was on the mountain, he made fun of the servants of Baal to the point that he had them in a fury. If

God had not sent the fire and confirmed His servant's faith, Elijah would have been torn to shreds. Elijah looked up and said, in effect, "God, either use me now or I'm coming up quick because they're tearing me apart." God sent the fire down on the altar.

Some are not in a place with God at all. They hang around the edges because they have never fully committed. The reason some people are such poor examples of Christianity is because they never had the door locked. You can get out anytime you want to and go back. Some conceal the sneaking idea that they may have to do that one of these days. You can walk with the Lord as long as things are normal, but when you get in a tight spot, it is nothing to fool with.

God revealed himself as fire. God is inscrutable and ineffable. He is those two things. You can't get at Him with your mind. This neo-rationalism passing for Christian theology and evangelicalism is trying to figure God out with our heads. And you can't do it. You can only experience God. God rises infinitely above the possibility of any man grasping Him intellectually.

God sets himself forth by figures and similitudes, and His favorite one seems to be fire. Remember God came to Israel as fire. The fire by night and the cloud by day. Later on, in the tabernacle, He dwelt between the wings of the cherubim as a fire. They call it the shekinah, the presence of God.

Then on Pentecost, when the Holy Ghost came upon those one hundred and twenty, He perpetuated that idea of God as fire, and each one of those disciples went out with a flame of fire on his forehead. The same fire, the presence of almighty God. Not some wild, irrational impulse, as some people believe.

The very presence of God is the fire, and now God wanted to show Moses who He was and bring him into experiencing an encounter with himself. If anybody is inclined to shy away from the word *experience*, I am not one of them. I believe in experience.

I define experience as a personal, conscious awareness of something by somebody. In our account, this somebody is Moses, and the Somebody that he was aware of is God. Moses wasn't unconscious when the burning bush happened, with it seeping through into his subconscious somehow. Rather, he was awake and aware of what was going on as he had an encounter with God that changed him, and he was never the same. Moses experienced God, and from that moment, God was no longer a theory. God was no longer knowledge by description, but now knowledge gained by experience or through personal acquaintance.

I am reminded of a story about the Scottish philosopher Thomas Carlyle (1795–1881), who was walking with a new minister in the garden. He linked his arm in the minister's arm and said, "Reverend, what this parish needs is somebody who knows God otherwise than by hearsay."

I'm convinced that many of us know God only by hearsay. He is what we want Him to be or hope that He is rather than what we know Him to be by spiritual encounter.

A tragic breakdown in evangelical circles is how we have used doctrine as a substitute for spiritual experience. Spiritual experience should be the outgrowth of doctrine. But we make doctrine terminal. And if we can recite the creed and know the notes in our study Bible, we think we are all set. But a lot of people stop right there and never go on to experience God. Bible doctrine is a highway to lead us to God, but there are many evangelicals asleep beside the highway. And because they're on the highway or near the highway, they call themselves evangelicals.

To me, an evangelical is somebody who not only believes the credo of the Christian but also experiences the God of the Christian. And there ought to be prophets in the day in which we live who are declaring that God can be experienced. That we can know God. That we don't have to make God a logical deduction from premises. That we can experience God as we can experience our children.

During one of my trips, my son met me with my four grandchildren at the airport. I could prove who they were by deduction, but when they grabbed me, I knew they were my grandchildren by experience.

I believe God can be known deep in the heart by spiritual experience. God wanted to say some things to Moses. And He did. He defeated Moses here, took all the self-confidence out of the man and beat him down and then raised him up. It's always God's way. Some of the things He taught Moses, He wants to teach us if we're going to be used at all of God.

One is that the fire dwelt in the bush, and the bush was at the mercy of the fire, that is it accepted the rule of the fire. You know when you hold a creed, that's all very well, but you'll never amount to anything until the creed holds you. As long as you hold the doctrine of God, that's all very well. It's better than being an atheist. But until God holds you and uses you as an extension of His own hands, you're not yet where you ought to be. And this is indicated here or taught us in the beautiful figure if not in a type, that the fire dwells in the bush.

I am a great believer in the indwelling Christ. As written in Colossians: "Christ in you, the hope of glory" (1:27). Not Christ with you only, though that's true. But Christ in you, which is the hope of glory. The problem of personality interpenetrating personality isn't a heavy one for me. I get blessed with lots of things that other people don't understand. And I admit I don't either, but they look good to me. And God blesses me, as the brother said, without much provocation. So, I get help. I get a lot of help, and there are a lot of problems I don't have.

An Anglican pastor came to me once and said, "Tozer, I'd like to ask you two questions. First, how do you explain the problem of the eternal God entering time? And the second one is, What is meant by the light that lighteth every man that comes into the world?"

I said, "Doctor, as for that first question, that isn't even a problem to me, how the eternal God can enter time and become flesh to dwell among us." So, I waved him off on that.

About the second question, I did have an opinion on that. But the problem of how personality interpenetrates personality was settled a long time ago by the iron in the fire. Put an iron in a fire and blow the old-fashioned bellows, and pretty soon you have fire in the iron. You do not have the loss of either personality. The iron is still the iron and the fire is still the fire, but you have them fused in experience. And if the fire goes out of the iron, you still have the two.

So, God enters the human breast, fuses His divine, uncreated personality with the created personality that is His child. They do not become metaphysically or ontologically one, but they become experientially one.

The fire, the glowing incandescence of God's presence in the breast of a man, becomes a little like God, so there's much of God in him and about him. And yet he is not God and God is not the man. Forever and forever, God remains God, and the man remains the man. And yet their personalities are united.

God was trying to say that to Moses, and He is saying that to us.

Revive Us Again

Revive us again;
Fill each heart with Thy love;
May each soul be rekindled
With fire from above.

—William P. MacKay (1839–
1885) / John J. Husband
(1760–1825)

CHAPTER 7

The Fire Transfigured the Bush

Moreover He said, "I am the God of your father—the God of Abraham, the God of Isaac, and the God of Jacob." And Moses hid his face, for he was afraid to look upon God.

—EXODUS 3:6

O Father, I praise You, that Your coming into my life was not because I am an important person. My significance comes solely from the fiery presence of the Holy Spirit in my life. Amen.

The bush was only a scrub thorn bush. I suppose millions were scattered over the broad face of the wilderness and did not amount to anything. They were like our acacia bushes and were not worth looking at twice.

The flame transfigured this particular bush until it became the most famous bush in all history. However, its glory was not its own; its glory was derived from the indwelling fire. It took on a glow, a glory, and held that glory all down through these years. People talk about the burning bush, an artist paints the burning bush, and we preach about the burning bush. Why? Because it was a great bush? No, because in it was a great fire.

Have you ever stopped to think that all the fungi and every bug and larvae and worms all perished in that burning bush? Not a single thing there but bush and fire.

I am not an expert in medicine. I read about the heatproof microbes that you can boil for two hours and still they do not die. However, nothing can stand raw fire; all life dies in the flame. There are evils within people that can stand the presence of revival meetings, religious meetings, and prayer meetings. No sin, however, can stand up under the presence of the indwelling God.

One byproduct of Christianity is that God takes ordinary people, and by living in them He transforms them, giving them meaning and significance.

Dwight L. Moody was a tongue-tied, uneducated shoe salesman. One day the Holy Ghost came on him in the streets of Philadelphia, and he went on his way a transfigured man.

I often think of my friend Thomas Haire, the praying plumber of Lisburn, Ireland. He used to put pipes together and say, "That will be four dollars." Tom had no formal education. So why, when you see him coming, do you know God is in the neighborhood? When he gets on his knees, you know that God is answering his prayer. Why do they talk about him all over Europe and America? Why do they write him letters by the hundreds asking for his prayer? Because God got in Thomas Haire and transfigured him. He was only an acacia bush and would have died and been forgotten with all the Irish acacia bushes of the Emerald Isle. But the Holy Ghost came and took him over.

The bush was transfigured by the flame. It had been only a scrub bush. Moses saw them by the hundreds, but this bush suddenly became the most famous bush in all history. Its glory was a derived glory. God did not make the bush great, He simply got in the bush and was great in the bush. So, everybody's attention was called to the bush.

Moses turned aside to see that transfigured bush, and it took on meaning. It got its significance there. It was related by nature to all the other acacia bushes, yet nobody ever talks about them. They all talk about that one bush, why? Because it had the fire in it.

One of the saddest things I know is the anonymity of the average man. Emerson said the average man and woman is only one more couple. Go out on the highways or down to the street corners or into the far jungle areas, wherever you will, east or west, north or south, you will find thousands of people crawling like animated clothespins over the face of the earth. They are born, have a bit of joy, and then die. They're faceless, without significance and meaning.

When Jesus Christ lays hold of a person, the first thing He does is to give him significance. He amounts to something. He gets a face. God dwells in the man and he becomes transfigured in the fire. And the faceless man touched by the Mighty Christ now takes on significance and meaning. The humblest new convert in the Baliem Valley of New Guinea is more in the kingdom of God than the Churchills and all of the rest of the great of the world because he has taken on a meaning that he never had before and that nobody can have except by the fire.

Breathe on Us, Lord of Life

Breathe on me, breath of God,
Till I am wholly Thine.
Until this earthly part of me
Glows with Thy fire divine.
—Edwin Hatch (1835–1889) /
Robert Jackson (1842?–1914)

CHAPTER 8

The Fire Protected the Bush

And God said to Moses, "I AM WHO I AM." And He said, "Thus you shall say to the children of Israel, 'I AM has sent me to you.'"

—EXODUS 3:14

O Father, where can I go to find the safety and security that is in You? I praise You for protecting me each day by the fiery presence of the Holy Spirit in my life. No evil can touch me because of You. Amen.

No evil could bother that bush as long as that fire was in it. Did you ever think that a hungry goat browsing at twilight never went near that bush? I am sure he checked other bushes, but he did not go near that one. And bugs undoubtedly were lighting around there but never lighted on that one. The bush was perfectly safe as long as the fire dwelt in it.

I believe in separation, but I do not believe in insulation. I do not believe it is the will of God for evangelical believers to insulate themselves from other people. If you will not interact with a non-Christian, how can you talk to him about the Lord? How are we going to help anybody, insulated like that? No, no. We are to be separated certainly, but we are not to isolate ourselves. We must remember that the fire is not at our discretion.

Monasticism was a historical error. They said, "I've got my fire, now I'm going to have to cup it and keep it." They cupped their hand around it, so the wind would not blow it out, then they went to the monastery. It was a great mistake. I honor them for their intention, but it does not speak too much for their knowledge of the Scriptures.

Simeon Stylites the Elder was the most horrible example of an effort to keep good by getting away from people. In the year AD 423, he got up on a pillar thirty feet high and stayed more than thirty years. There he was, and he never came down even to take a bath. Never came down for anything. He thought he was being holy. Friends fed him up there. I would have starved him down if I had it to do myself, but they pulled food up by a rope.

The Son of God, who walked among men, publicans, and sinners, talked at the well to a fallen woman, was holy and pure because the purity was inside of Him. We become pure and safe by the indwelling fire. We do not become safe by hiding.

I am not very fond of flying. Perhaps I was born thirty years too early. However, there are times that I have to fly. Recently, I flew out of what they call a gray drizzle. As I walked up to the plane, I said, "Now, Lord, I'm in your hands. It's either Chicago or glory. One or the other."

I have every reason to believe that a man or a woman is perfectly safe while the fire of God's presence dwells in him. Nobody can hurt a Christian. Nobody can get through to a Christian unless the Lord wants him to. When the devil wanted to tempt Job, he said, "God, you've got a hedge around the man." He had to ask permission to get through. God opened the hedge, and the devil slipped through and went in to tempt him. So, no child of God can be injured if he has the fire dwelling in him.

What was it that protected the bush? It was the fire. If it had happened today, we would have held a four-day meeting and talked and gossiped and then passed some resolutions to build a wire fence around the bush so nobody would bother it. That bush did not need any wire fence or glass encasing, because nobody bothered the bush while the fire was in it.

As I said earlier, there was not a goat anywhere in all Asia Minor that would dare come up and smell that bush. He did not get near enough because his nose would have been burned with the heat. So, he stayed away, perfectly safe.

A Christian does not have to defend himself. Some ought to practice unclosing their fists; unclose them. You might have been a fighter all your life. Anybody who says anything against you, you are ready to rise up, write them a hot letter and say, "What do you mean? You're attacking my character?" Imagine that bush had been writing letters, saying, "They're attacking me."

Nobody attacked the bush; they could not because the bush was perfectly safe while the fire dwelled in it. If a buzzard circled overhead looking for a place to light in the twilight, it would not light on that bush. Its feathers would have been singed off very quickly because there was a fire in that bush. Safety lies not in constitutions, bylaws, regulations, and church order, but in the presence of God in the midst.

If God dwells in the church, that church is a safe church. That is why I never join groups that want to go to Washington, DC, and fight for the church. I never would join the Ecumenical-minded brethren who want to go and be represented before Congress.

We have God in our midst, and when we have a fire in the bush, we are safe and the church is safe—safe by the Holy Ghost.

All Creatures of Our God and King

Thou flowing water, pure and clear,
Make music for thy Lord to hear.
Alleluia! Alleluia!

Thou fire so masterful and bright,
Thou givest man both warmth and light!
O praise Him, O praise Him!
Alleluia! Alleluia! Alleluia!

—St. Francis of Assisi (1181/82–1226) /
William H. Draper (1855–1933)

CHAPTER 9

That Bush Became Beautiful in the Fire

And let the beauty of the LORD our God be upon
us, and establish the work of our hands for us; yes,
establish the work of our hands.

—PSALM 90:17

*O God our Father, I seek You that I may know You in the beauty
of Your sacred revelation. May Your fire burn within me and
clear out anything that hinders that beauty in me. Amen.*

The old Greek philosophers, for all their facts, had no revelation. Sometimes in their blindness they blundered close to the truth. They believed beauty was a part of truth somehow and was near God. They believed that somewhere was a central virtue, and that because we are intellectual, there was a central intellect. And they believed there was a central beauty somewhere.

Moses knew there was. He said, "Let the beauty of the Lord our God be upon us." And here was an acacia bush that nobody would have brought home and planted in his yard. It had no beauty but now was beautiful because it was aglow. The old hymn says, "Stay oh beauty uncreated, ever ancient, ever new." The beauty of God was there. When Jesus came down to become man, His garments smelled of myrrh and aloes and cassia, straight out of the ivory palaces.

You are called to be a burning bush. This is the world's sundown, and there are people like Moses, alone, looking for somebody that looks like God. Somebody who has fire in him. A lonely person somewhere may be looking in your direction.

Unlovely Christianity has done more to turn people away from Christ than all the liberalism in the world. I am an evangelical, and if you strain it a little, stretch it, and put a few footnotes around it, I am even a fundamentalist. I am an essentialist, and a believer in historic Christianity, the faith of our Fathers, which is living still. Yet until evangelical Christianity gets through and meets God in the fire and gets God burning and glowing within, we are going to have all these troubles and are not going to solve them by meetings and conferences. I am sorry, but I cannot believe that we are going to solve them. For it is not techniques to follow or methods to be followed, it is Christ and His Father—God and the man in God and God in the man. The fire of the Holy Ghost will burn through an awful lot of problems that he would not be able to solve in a thousand panel discussions.

Where are the saints today? Do you feel a desire to be one? The strange and wonderful thing is when you are one, you do not know it. That bush did not know anything about its attractiveness. There it was, just burning away and did not know it. The great saints did not know they were saints. They would smile, scold you, and chase you away if you told them they were saints; they did not believe it, but they were. The beauty of Jesus dwelt in them.

We are not called to be great. We are not called to be beautiful. It may be beautiful in the fire, but not in your boldness or courage. Our call should be to be a burning bush. My recommendation to those who feel called to God's work is to shun the coarse ways of the cheap gospellers and amateurs, bringing the spirit of the marketplace and the bank and the entertainment into the church. Shun them, stay away from them.

I heard the president of a Bible college in a serious talk say that we are suffering in evangelical circles an epidemic of amateurism. Anybody can get up and talk. Oh, the amateurism, the coarseness, the ignorance, the cheap humor, not a flash of wit sometimes to wake an audience, but cheap clowning. I say shun it and stay away from it.

We already have enough promoters; we need prophets. We already have enough organizers; we need men and women who have met God in the crisis of encounter. We have enough converted pugilists to draw crowds to see them flex their biceps; we need people in whom the fire burns.

The sanest person today is one who knows God the most; the sanest mind in the world is one in which the fire dwells the most perfectly.

When you talk about the fire that dwells in the bush and the glory of God and the sweetness of the Lord high and lifted up, the world says, "He's crazy." You are talking perfectly well, but the world doesn't understand your language, which is why people think you are a little off. However, the beautiful part about it is, afterward, they generally come around to you.

Maybe this is the most important for us in our work as believers. That bush became beautiful in the fire. Moses many years later wrote, "Let the beauty of the Lord our God be upon us." I wonder if Moses was not thinking of the beauty of God in that bush, that solemn, wonderful hour when he saw God and met Him in the fire.

Augustine of Hippo wrote in *Confessions*:

Late have I loved you, O Beauty ever ancient, ever new, late have I loved you! You were within me, but I was outside, and it was there that I searched for you. In my unloveliness, I plunged into the lovely things which you created. You were with me, but I was not with you. Created things kept me from you; yet if they had not been in you they would have not

75

been at all. You called, you shouted, and you broke through my deafness. You flashed, you shone and you dispelled my blindness. You breathed your fragrance on me; I drew in a breath and now I pant for you. I have tasted you, now I hunger and thirst for more. You touched me, and I burned for your peace.

As I wrote earlier, the fire Moses encountered purified the bush, and the bugs and larva all perished. The fire burnt their whole business.

As a farm boy, I know there are many free boarders on the average bush. There are all kinds of life, from the fungus and all sorts of bugs and worms under the leaves, to the larva or unhatched worms. There they are, but turn a fire loose on that bush for five minutes, and after that there is not a living thing left in the bush. And there would not have been a bush if God had not preserved it. The fire preserved the bush through it all. No one can stand before the fire of God's presence, as no living thing can stand in fire.

God is the holiness that we need. Some people think holiness is something you get and take out with you and guard it lest you lose it. No, holiness is nothing less than the holy God dwelling in a human heart, and the heart will be holy because God is there. The bush had no purity of its own. When the fire went out in that bush, no doubt before the next day, other bugs were back again.

I believe the presence of God burning in the human breast purifies that breast. As long as it burns unhindered, those evils that used to follow us around and were part of our personality will be burned away, and there will be nothing but white ash to show where they used to be.

Nothing can stand raw fire. All life dies before the flame. There are evils in the breast, but none can stand the presence of revival and prayer meetings. No sins can stand up under the presence of the indwelling God.

I suppose if we were to pass around a questionnaire and ask people to define *sanctification*, we would get countless definitions. For that reason, I cannot possibly allow myself to get involved in doctrinal disputes over the word. But I believe that God wants His people to be holy. I do believe that. I do not believe holiness is ever separated from God. God is holy and only God is holy. And where God is, there is holiness, and where God is not, there is just us. And there is no one who can try to make it any other way, except as the bush that was purified by the fire.

Search Me, O God

I praise Thee, Lord,
For cleansing me from sin;
Fulfill Thy Word,
And make me pure within.
Fill me with fire
Where once I burned with shame;
Grant my desire
To magnify Thy name.

—J. Edwin Orr (1912–1987)

CHAPTER 10

The Walls Concealing God's Presence

Restore us, O God of hosts; cause Your face to shine, and we shall be saved!

—PSALM 80:7

O God, it is Your face I earnestly seek each day. Hide not Your face from me. Let me come into Your presence and enjoy Your smiling face toward me. Amen.

D o not let anything or anybody lead you away from the glorious knowledge of God's face.

As a Christian, the smiling face of God is turned toward you. The question is, why do we not enjoy that relationship? Why, as Christians, are we not capturing the wondrous divine illumination of our Savior, the Lord Jesus Christ? Why do we not feel the divine fire in our hearts, strive to sense and experience the feeling of our reconciliation with God, as well as the knowledge of it? Why do we not gain possession of it?

The reason is, between us and the smiling face of God is a wall of obscurity.

There is never such a thing as a day when the sun does not shine. There are dark days, misty days, and days that get so dark you have to turn on the lights. Yes, there are dark days, and yet the sun is shining just as brightly as on the brightest, clearest day in June. Why then does it not shine on the earth? Because there is between the sun and the earth a wall of obscurity. The sun is all right and is up there grinning broadly, just as bright and hot and radiant as ever, but it does not get through to the earth because of a wall of obscurity.

How can we define this wall of obscurity? We know what it is from the standpoint of the weather, but how does it apply to Christians?

This wall of obscurity is the wall we allow to be over us as Christians. What is this wall? Atonement has been made; there is nothing for us to do for it has all been done. Not another drop of blood needs to be shed, not a spear needs to enter the holy heart, not a tear nor groan nor a drop of sweat. Not a moment of agony, death has no more dominion over us; it is done, it is finished forever. The face of God shines down upon us.

So, what is that wall? It may be one thing, it may be many things, but one wall is self-will.

Self-will is a very religious thing. It may enter right with you into the church when you join and with you into the chamber when you pray, yet it is self-will. Self-will is good-natured only when it is getting its own way. It is grouchy and ill-tempered when crossed.

Is your surrender to God sufficient so you can be spiritual even when crossed?

Another wall is ambition, even religious ambition. People are religiously ambitious for something, perhaps not in the will of God, but for self-aggrandizement. The result is a wall above them, between them and their God.

I am not just writing about this for others. Ambition is something I have had to give up myself. I must be ready at any moment to give up my pastorate and let it ride away on any sermon I preach or any position I take. My job as editor of the *Alliance Weekly*, my position in the religious world, everything has to be on the chopping block and ready to go. If I own it, it is a wall over my head, and it becomes a wall of obscurity that nothing will penetrate. People try to pray through, but you cannot pray through it, nothing can penetrate it. There are those who try to fast their way through, and it cannot be done.

This modern idea that if you pray long enough everything will be okay is just not right. In 1 Samuel 16, we find Samuel praying for King Saul, whom God had already rejected. God essentially puts His hand over Samuel's mouth, and says, "Samuel, don't pray anymore for Saul, don't pray for him."

Another instance is in Joshua 7, when Joshua is lying facedown, praying. God tells him, "What is the use of lying there on your stomach? I don't honor a man lying on his belly. Get up and deal with the situation and your wall, and then I'll bless you and save all that is lying around you groaning."

The idea that we can pray the wall away while we are hanging on to our ambitions, that is our trouble.

Another wall is called fear.

Fear is always a child of unbelief, no matter what you are scared about, whether it is fear that you have cancer, your child is sick, you may lose your job, or the possibility that war will break out. Fear over your head is a wall of obscurity and hides God's smiling face from you.

Another wall is self-love.

We might make a joke out of this, but we never should because self-love is a wall of obscurity. Even the Christian who has offered himself to Christ, has believed and is converted, can keep the wall of obscurity over him simply by loving himself. To fall out of love with yourself hurts you like falling off something. Other self-sins are self-aggrandizement and self-admiration, and as long as they remain there will be a wall of obscurity.

Another wall is money.

Money these days gets between God and us and can cause some really serious problems.

An evangelist years ago pointed out that it takes only two dimes to block your view of the landscape. Take two dimes with you to the great Smoky Mountains. Go clear up to the top, and hold a dime close in front of your eyes. The mountains will still be there smiling in the sun, but you will not see them because there is a dime in front of each eye. It does not take much money. We who don't have much money always make snide remarks at rich people. But you can be rich and only have ten dollars because, if it is between you and your God, that wall is concealing you from God.

Another wall is people.

The Lord tells us that we should not be afraid of man with his breath in his nostrils. Yet there are Christians who have a wall of fear above them constantly because they want to fit into society. They are afraid of standing apart. If fitting into society is your goal, you have a wall over your heart. The Word of God should define the church, not society.

Then there are friends and positions and loved ones, and this is perhaps the hardest, that they all have to go. You say, "And then what do I do with this? If this wall is over my head as a wall of obscurity and my Father is smiling at me and I can't see His face, what shall I do?"

He calls it the wall of forgetting. He said to put this wall that is above you under your feet and there will be a wall of forgetting.

It was the apostle Paul who said, "Brethren, I do not count myself to have apprehended; but one thing I do, forgetting those things which are behind and reaching forward to those things which are ahead" (Philippians 3:13). For Paul, "those things" were a wall between him and God, but he put them behind him. His defeats, mistakes, blunders, errors, wrongs, the times he fell on his face, and the time the Lord dealt with him for his pride, and all of this was put behind him and under his feet as a wall of forgetting.

The job of Christians is to get this wall of forgetting under our feet. Some understand and will do something about it. Others are not going to understand and, like the Israelites, will turn back to the wilderness and wonder why there is sand in their shoes. Remember that God is still smiling and waiting for you within the veil, or to change the figure of speech, He is waiting for you to move up.

Now put this under your feet: money, people, friends, position, loved ones, fear, all that I claim and call my own, ambitions, pride, stubbornness, self-will, and anything else the Holy Spirit may point to in my life. Whatever rival there is, it is a wall between God and me. I do not say we are not joined to Him. I do not say we are not justified. I say this wondrous divine illumination, this ability to perfectly love Him and worthily praise Him has been choked out, smitten down, and taught out of us for generations. This we lack because we will not put under our feet the wall of obscurity. We let it rise between our God and us. If we put all of this under us, we will find it hides all of our past and all that has bothered us and all that has shamed us and worries us and grieves us; it is down there and out and gone, and there's nothing but the clear sky above.

Christ does not have to die again. No cross needs ever to be erected again. No value needs to be added to the atonement, the face of God smiles on His people, even though the walls hide Him.

Jesus walked among men in that day with eyes bright and His vision keen. He said to them, "Whatever they tell you, do because they're theologically right, but don't be like them." And they said, "We will kill that man," and they did kill Him. But He rose on the third day and sent down the Holy Ghost into the world and He is mine and yours: He is our sweet possession.

Do not let anybody tell you how much you can have. Only God can tell you how much you can have. Don't let anybody take you aside and tell you not to get excited, not to get fanatical because you got all there is. Don't let any of that happen to you.

Just as sure as God lives, if we continue in the direction we've been moving in evangelical circles, that which is now fundamentalism will become liberalism in a short time. We have to have the Holy Spirit back and we have to have the face of God shining down. The candles of our soul are burning bright. To sense and feel and know the wondrous divine illumination of Him who said, "I am the light of the world," does that make a fanatic out of you? Come on, let us little fanatics just go out and be joyful in the Lord.

If that is fanaticism, what a sweet fanatic it makes out of a man; what a happy wonder it is to be fanatic. No, that is not really fanaticism. It is fanaticism when you revolt against the Scriptures, imagine things, do weird things, and misinterpret the Word of God. If you are willing to put that wall of self and self-love and fear and stubbornness and pride and greed and ambition under your feet, then there is nothing for you to do. All has been done, you cannot climb to heaven on a rope ladder, there is nothing left for you to do.

I Take, He Undertakes

I clasp the hand of Love divine,
I claim the gracious promise mine,
And add to His my countersign,
"I take"—"He undertakes."

—A. B. Simpson (1843–1919)

CHAPTER 11

Connecting with the Burning Bush

While we do not look at the things which are seen,
but at the things which are not seen. For the things
which are seen are temporary, but the things which
are not seen are eternal.

—2 CORINTHIANS 4:18

O Father, I praise You that You have revealed Yourself unto my heart. My eyes are not equal to Your presence. Fill my heart with Your presence every day. Amen.

It doesn't take a great deal of intelligence to know that Paul, the man of God who spoke as he was moved by the Holy Ghost, is contrasting two kinds of seeing. He did not advise us to try to see the invisible with our naked eye. No, it is the external eye that sees the visible and the internal eye that sees the invisible. Paul says there is a gazing, a looking, that has to be done with the inward eye and not with the external.

Life all about us is charged with mystery. All the quality in life comes from the mysterious part of it. The part that can be explained does not fully explain the part of life truly to be valued. We can study anatomy and biology and know all about children and babies. But that doesn't explain why people love babies. There isn't any explanation. You can paint, write poetry, and orate until you're blue in the face, and yet there is an overtone, a rainbow of emotional color about it all that makes babies precious to us. And so it is with almost everything. There is a glory in imponderable things, instinctive things, things that are unlearned. They give meaning to life. The glory of our lives, that for which we live, lies in the intangibles, the things we can see only with the inward eye.

Take two men, for instance, a farmer and an artist, who take a little walk to see their friends on an October afternoon.

The farmer sees the corn and fat cattle and will talk pleasantly about having to bring in his machine and how it's about time to shift a hundred head to another field. What he sees is what you can buy and sell, put in the boxcar, and evaluate in terms of dollars and cents.

All the time on the same walk, the artist is thrilled. He sees the cattle, but he doesn't know how much they cost. He sees the corn but has no idea of its value. What he sees can't be measured or bought nor sold, but nevertheless gives value to living in the world.

The farmer is fixing it so he can physically live in the world by having milk and meat and vegetables. But the other man says, "Yes, you make it possible for us to live in the world. But *why* live in the world?" The blue sky and fleecy clouds and colored leaves tell him why.

You can't explain or write a book on, Is life worth living? It either is or it isn't. Everybody knows it is the one who has felt the thrill of love and known the glory who belongs to God. You can't prove it; you just know it.

Take a dog who may be running out into the night and may for a moment take a quick casual glance at the starry sky. Dogs have eyes and sight; they have good eyes and they can see well. The dog sees the moon hanging there and he sees the stars. But what does he do about it? Nothing at all. He's looking for an animal that he may pull down and eat. But he does see the stars.

David talks about the stars by night, the moon, and heavens above, and what they tell about God forever, singing as they shine—the hand that made this is divine.

Both eyes saw the heavens, but the eyes of the dog saw nothing. The eyes of the spiritually inspired poet David saw the wonder and the glory of it all. It is the intangible thing, the thing you don't learn that's there because you're human, and God made you and stamped you with the royal imagery of himself.

There is another world than this, but this isn't it. You can have all this and lose your own soul and be nobody. Certainly, it is the very essence of the Old and New Testament. And yet busy men have not taken this very seriously. They reverse the apostle's text that says, "The things that are seen are temporal, but the things that are unseen are eternal" and they've reversed it and edited it a bit. And while they would agree that this is true, in their living they prove that when they quote it, they mean it like this: "For the things that are invisible and unseen are rather shaky and unreal. But the things you see, they are the real things."

They turned the attention of people from God to earth and from heaven above to this veil of suffering and woe. And they put their emphasis upon the things that can be seen, and they said, "Don't talk to us about invisible things." They talk to us about things we can get our teeth into. Like how we want to have more. Want to have bigger cars, bigger farms, better cattle. Women and men want to dress better. We want to be paid more and we want to work shorter hours. Don't talk to us about heaven. We want to know about earth.

This reminds me of what Paul said,

However, we speak wisdom among those who are mature, yet not the wisdom of this age, nor of the rulers of this age, who are coming to nothing. But we speak the wisdom of God in a mystery, the hidden wisdom which God ordained before the ages for our glory, which none of the rulers of this age knew; for had they known, they would not have crucified the Lord of glory. But as it is written: "Eye has not seen, nor ear heard, nor have entered into the heart of man the things which God has prepared for those who love Him." But God has revealed them to us through His Spirit. For the Spirit searches all things, yes, the deep things of God.

—1 Corinthians 2:6–10

And here we break away from the, "Give us more of this now. Give us what we can see and weigh and measure and feel and touch." We rise to the wisdom that says, "I must have something to see and hear and touch." I'm a human being. God has given me a body that, like a car, has to be gassed up occasionally. I have to recharge it sometimes, and so I will not despise God's humble gift of pumpkins and corn and fat cattle. I won't despise it, but I will only say these that are seen are temporal, whereas the things not seen are eternal.

The woe of the world has been its bondage to visible things. Afflicting men in all parts of the world at all times, not only religions, but philosophers themselves who were not particularly religious, held this to be the prime curse of the world that we are victims of the things that we can see. We have allowed ourselves to be chained down to visible things, and it's a great error to hold that visible things are the ultimate reality. They are not but are evanescent, passing, as a shadow across the meadow on a cloudy day, of things not seen, eternal. The things that are seen are the balls and chains on the ankles of the human race and hold us back so we can't fly, not allowing our feeble wings will not lift us up.

When I talk about mysticism, which is only the word of God, I am not asking anybody to look at a dream world.

I don't believe in a dream world or an imaginary world. I don't believe in anything imaginary. I want to be able when I talk about a thing to go and say, "Look, there it is, that's what I'm talking about."

When Scripture says that faith is the evidence of things not seen, faith is not a place where you go and hide. It is not a retreat from reality. It is a gateway to reality where we see the real things. We are not asking anybody to accept imaginative or imaginary things. We are asking them to build their faith on that which is. Abraham saw a city that had a foundation whose builder and maker was God, but Abraham never saw it with his external eyes. He saw it with his inner eyes. That was not an imaginary thing. We are not asking him to become dreamy and write silly poetry about it. We ask him, "Abraham, look, there's a city. Look quick—you won't see it long. There it is. You're a busy man, and you'll only get a glimpse, but there it is." Abraham looked quickly and saw it with his inner eyes.

Somebody said after that he never would live in the city; instead he lived in a tent. He couldn't stand any city after he'd seen that one by comparison. So instead of ghosts and fairies, we believe in reality. God reveals the real world, with its substance. And it can't be seen with the outward eye, but it can be experienced with the inward eye. And it is the only ultimate reality.

I am made to wonder at the wisdom of the Christian. We ought not to gaze with awe and wonder at great minds. The apostle Paul called them the "rulers of this age" (1 Corinthians 2:6). And Paul himself was one of the greatest minds in history. Yet we need not go to the great minds of our generation to help us understand God or His Word.

The Christian has wisdom, but not of this world. A Christian penetrates, passes through, sees, touches, and handles things unseen. He has learned to distinguish that which has value from that which has no value. He has learned the correct table by which he judges things. So he no longer wastes his money.

The Christian has learned what's real and what isn't real. The worldling doesn't know shadow from substance. Sometimes he will give his life to a shadow and find at the end that he's missed the substance. But a Christian knows where substance is. God has given him X-ray eyes, he can see through the shadows, and he won't waste his time on shadows nor talents nor money nor efforts. And the Christian has found the everlasting reality. And I tell you I don't know what it is in my heart. But I assume it's in everybody's, but I could never let myself rest unless I knew eternity was in this thing. I'm not going to be around here long, and neither are you, for us to give our time to that which we can't keep.

Did not the devil say to Jesus, "All this I will give you and the glory of it, for it is mine and I can give it to whom I will"? Jesus with not one penny in His pocket, not one dime in the bank said, "Get thee behind me, Satan." The Lord Jehovah, Him only shall I serve.

We live for the unseen, for God, for Christ, for the Holy Ghost.

Every man must die and come to judgment. And if there's nothing beyond that, then I refuse to be concerned, I absolutely refuse. Jesus Christ came to Judaism, and He found a religion in meats and drinks and carnal ordinances. It had a heart and a soul and a spirit, but it also had many external examples and shadows of heavenly things.

96

Jesus Christ our Lord swept all the shadows away, brought life and immortality to light through the gospel and projected the eternal into the temporal and the everlasting into the passing, and said, "I go to prepare a place for you. . . . That where I am, there you may be also." He talked about it as a man talks about the house that he bought or the farm that he owns; it was real. But He said it is a spiritual thing and swept away the shadows. He said God is spirit and that we may worship Him in spirit and in truth.

Jesus Christ came to a Judaism that was locked in those things and swept them all away. He said the kingdom of heaven is within you, and if you worship God, you must worship Him in spirit and in truth, and where two or three are gathered in His name there is your church. But He allowed us two visible symbols: bread and wine. Bread to tell of my broken body, He said, and wine to tell of my shed blood. And as often as you meet together, the world wonders what you're doing and peeks in to see and they see you eating the bread and drinking the wine, and you're thinking of me.

So, for the weak that can't quite get things, but whose faith demands a little prop from the outside, He said, all right, bread and wine I give you this. I'll give you this now. As often as you do it, you do it in remembrance of me. But in itself it is nothing. It is what it stands for, what it symbolizes. It is the ring on the finger of the bride to remind her that her bridegroom is in the glory waiting for her. These symbols tell it—realities that are eternal.

My God, How Wonderful Thou Art

My God, how wonderful Thou are,
Your majesty, how bright;
How beautiful Thy mercy seat,
In depths of burning light!
—Frederick William Faber
(1814–1863)

CHAPTER 12

Dwelling in the Secret Place of the Most High

He who dwells in the secret place of the Most High
shall abide under the shadow of the Almighty.

—PSALM 91:1

Your word, O God, is a lamp unto our feet. Lead us and guide us today at this moment in the path of Your choosing. Help us to find that secret place and dwell there in the safety and security of Your presence. In Jesus' name, amen.

I'm not sure if Moses wrote Psalm 91, but I need to include it in this book because if he did write it, I believe the psalm is a demonstration of what his life was like following the burning-bush experience.

What Moses is trying to get across in Psalm 91 is the idea that being in God's presence is not a one-time experience and then we walk away. From that moment on, Moses walked in the secret place of the Most High. He walked in the presence of God.

The bush was not God. The fire was not God. God was in the bush and the fire, but that was only for a moment in time. Following that, Moses had within him the presence of God wherever he went.

This explains why Moses' courage and fearlessness were used of God to lead Israel out of Egypt. This was the reason he was able to stand up to Pharaoh and all of the Egyptians and not back down.

I believe what God wants us to understand is that when we encounter Him and experience His presence, it is a life-changing experience and we will never be the same. It will enable us to do for God what only God can do through us.

Moses starts this song out with, "He who dwells in the secret place of the Most High shall abide under the shadow of the Almighty." This is quite important and explains a lot of Moses' life. We are walking and living and existing under God's presence, under the shadow of the Almighty. We are not walking in darkness, but in the shadow of the Almighty that separates and keeps us away from the world around us. The world can see us, but the world can't really see us. We are in the shadow of the Almighty and live under His protection.

In verse two, Moses says, "I will say of the LORD, 'He is my refuge and my fortress; my God; in Him I will trust." This was the consequence of that burning-bush experience with God's presence, and now his refuge was in God.

I often wonder what Moses thought about leading up to the burning-bush experience during those forty years out in the mountains taking care of sheep all day long and looking at the stars at night. What was going through his mind? We don't know, but I think his mind changed forever when he encountered God at that burning bush. His mind now was on God. God was his refuge. God was his fortress. If that is true, Moses feared nobody. Whatever God wanted him to do, he was going to do.

The reason Moses left Egypt was because he was afraid. He feared the Egyptians and even his own people, the Israelites. Fear drove him into the mountains far away from Egypt. He wanted to do something for God's people, Israel, but fear kept him away.

That burning-bush experience burned fear out of his life forever and put inside him courage that only can come from understanding and knowing God. I think Moses gives his testimony in verses three and four: "Surely He shall deliver you from the snare of the fowler and from the perilous pestilence. He shall cover you with His feathers, and under His wings you shall take refuge; His truth shall be your shield and buckler."

What a wonderful testimony these first several verses are. I think that being covered under the shadow is a very important thing. Moses talks about that quite a bit, and the inference is that wherever I go, God is over me and protecting me; God is keeping away from me that which would harm me. Now, the secret to all of this is to cultivate God's presence on a daily, moment-by-moment basis. I think that was the secret of Moses' life.

He just didn't encounter God at the burning bush and then after that give a testimony something like, "Oh, I remember the day when I met God in the burning bush." Too many of our testimonies are based on things that happened years ago. Moses' testimony was based upon the presence of God in his life right now.

I could be wrong, but I don't think Moses talked about his burning-bush experience. I don't know that anybody knew about it except Moses, because he was the one we think wrote about it, and it does not seem like something he would go back to and back to and back to. He went forward in the power and demonstration of the Holy Spirit. Upon leaving the burning-bush experience, Moses went into a world that was totally against him.

Remember when he returned to Egypt with his brother Aaron? Even the Israelites were not in favor of him. They were afraid of Moses because they thought he was responsible for much of their suffering. Of course, Egypt did not remember him anymore, so he had no influence there. People who had known him in his younger years were long gone. Forty years had passed, but Egypt didn't want anything to do with him, including the current Pharaoh, who tried to challenge him several times. But Moses always stood his ground because he was living under the shadow of the Almighty, and nothing could frighten him. Nothing could turn him away.

Moses says in verses nine and ten, "Because you have made the LORD, who is my refuge, even the Most High, your dwelling place, no evil shall befall you, nor shall any plague come near your dwelling." Remember the plagues that God sent to Egypt through Moses to force Pharaoh to let the Israelites go? None of those plagues touched God's people, because God's people at that time were under the umbrella of Moses, who was under the umbrella of the Most High God. God sent Moses fully qualified and equipped to protect Israel from Egypt and to lead Israel into the Canaan land God had promised Abraham so many years before.

I cannot imagine how much Moses endured during that time. Even when he left Egypt and brought Israel across the river and into Canaan, he put up with all of the bickering and complaining of the Israelites. I think this was possible because he was dwelling in God's presence.

Remember when Moses came down from the mountain with the Ten Commandments? His face was so aglow that people could not even look at him. He did not know his face was aglow, but the same fire that was in the burning bush was now on his face, and he had to shelter it from the Israelites.

Walking with Moses would have been a challenge for those who did not understand and believe what God was doing.

Moses knew that God was going to use him to do that which could not be done any other way. God sent Moses, and in that sending dwelt the presence of God, moment by moment. I would have liked to have talked to Moses and have him tell me a little about what it was like during those times—what it was like to walk in God's presence and have no fear, going forward in the way of hope and faith.

Our faith depends upon the active presence of God in our life. "Faith comes by hearing, and hearing by the word of God." If we have faith, it is because there is the presence in us, the presence of God that will change everything about our life.

Many people have faith, but not the kind Moses had, which came by basking in God's presence. When we begin to walk in that presence, nothing else really matters. I long to be in the presence of God day after day, and I long to have His presence energize my life.

Our physical life is so limited, but God's presence is un-limited. His presence lifts us above all of our problems and difficulties. Find your burning-bush experience, and then go forward daily in the presence of the Lord, under the shadow of the Almighty. All the resources you need for what God wants you to do are in His secret place.

Eternal Father

O Trinity of love and power,
Our brethren shield in danger's hour;
From Rock and tempest, fire and foe,
Protect them wheresoever they go;
Thus evermore shall rise to Thee,
Glad praise from air and land and sea.

—William Whiting (1825–1878) /
John Bacchus Dykes (1823–1876) /
Robert Nelson Spencer (1877–1861)

CHAPTER 13

The Need for a Definitive Experience

Then the priests who bore the ark of the covenant of the LORD stood firm on dry ground in the midst of the Jordan; and all Israel crossed over on dry ground, until all the people had crossed completely over the Jordan.

—JOSHUA 3:17

Eternal Father of our Lord and Savior, Jesus Christ, I praise You for the grace You have given me to experience You for myself. Thank You for Your presence in my life each day. Amen.

Joshua 3 tells us how the Israelites crossed the Jordan River to enter the promised land, Canaan. They completely crossed over a sharp line to get there. A crisis had peaked in the past—an event had occurred. That is the way God works. There was a time when there was no creation, and then God created the heaven and the earth. An event had taken place. Crises had passed, heaven and earth were created. Man was created, but then he was fallen.

You can go through the Scriptures and find clear lines of demarcation when there was an occurrence and then things became different. After the event come goals and development and conquests. But unless the event has taken place, there cannot be growth. If there has been no birth, there can be no growth. If there was no crossing over the river, there can be no conquest of the land beyond. Always it must be after the event.

After crossing the Jordan and its water returned, Joshua instructed the people to set up a monument. The riverbed stones used were literally taken from the experience itself.

The stones, likely round because stones found in rivers usually do not have sharp edges, were evidently large enough to create a monument. And they were not simply dumped on the ground, but carefully formed into some kind of a permanent monument.

If anyone asked why the stones were there, in so many words, Joshua said, "Tell them this is a memorial to an event. It symbolizes something that took place, a crisis that passed, so you and future generations can remember what occurred here."

There's too much unclear Christianity. I believe the difference between revival and that half-dead state most of us find ourselves in can be attributed to the clarity and the sharpness of experience. The definitive crisis experience that some people have as revival mounts is a target to shoot for, something to expect. That neighbor of yours? There was an event, and he became a Christian. Or he was a spiritually dead kind of a Christian, and then something happened to him in the fullness of the Holy Ghost, and he became a live, spiritual Christian. We need an event, a crisis, that leads to revival. I believe this is our difficulty now.

Without an inward spiritual experience, a person is not in the Christian faith. He is only a camp follower, not a true Christian. The experience is a conscious awareness of something by somebody.

I don't believe in "unconscious" Christianity. I do not believe that anything you get from God in the realm of redemption comes to you subconsciously. Nobody goes to bed and wakes up in the morning and finds he's a Christian. The true Christian is consciously aware that God is there and has forgiven his sins and spoken to his heart. That's conscious awareness.

The reasonable conclusion I gather about the children of Israel passing through the Jordan is that they knew its significance. It was a dramatic and colorful experience. They knew when they were in the river, knew when they'd gotten to the other side, knew it was the time and place to put up a monument, and then they marked it as a sign of a clear spiritual event in their lives.

If you are not consciously aware an experience took place, I conclude it didn't happen. That sounds reasonable to me.

Nobody is consecrated unless he knows he has been consecrated. Take, for example, a soldier out fighting the enemy. One day he finds himself surrounded, weapons turned in his direction, and men yelling for him to surrender. He drops his gun, raises both hands, and surrenders. As long as he maintains his memory, he will remember that moment. Likewise, when General Robert E. Lee turned over his sword to the Northern General Ulysses S. Grant, and General Grant handed it back, Lee was consciously aware of his surrender.

If you have not consciously surrendered to the Lord, you have not surrendered to Him.

I imagine that when the Israelites gathered with their twelve stones, the leader representing Judah threw a stone down and said, "This is mine." And the leader of the tribe of Reuben brought his stone, and the others brought theirs and put them down there and each said, "Now, here's my rock," representing the twelve tribes.

When their enemies heard the Lord had dried up the waters of the Jordan, allowing Israel to cross over, they did just what God said they would do. Joshua 5:1 says the enemies' "heart melted; and there was no spirit in them any longer." We would say their morale had sunk, but Scripture says their collective heart melted, which I think is a much nicer way to say it.

For the Israelites, their obstacles began to melt away and victories began to be won because they had crossed over the

Jordan consciously, put down their stones, and declared, "We're over that line."

God Leads Us Along

Some thro' the waters,
Some thro' the flood,
Some thro' the FIRE,
But all thro' the blood;
Some thro' great sorrow,
But God gives a song,
In the night season,
And all the day long.

—G. A. Young
(1855–1935)

CHAPTER 14

The Bush before Which We Kneel

"Again I say to you that if two of you agree on earth concerning anything that they ask, it will be done for them by My Father in heaven. For where two or three are gathered together in My name, I am there in the midst of them."

—MATTHEW 18:19–20

It is such a privilege to gather together among those who also are enjoying the presence of God. In our fellowship, O Father, Your presence is indeed cherished and appreciated. Amen.

I f any church is a real church, it is a communion, not an institution merely organized and established. Anybody can set up a church, get a pastor, elect a board. But unless that institution is also a communion, it is not a New Testament church.

A New Testament church must be a company of people drawn together with the fascination—the desire—to seek God, to feel God, to hear God, to be where God is. As the Greeks approached their sacred place and as the Jews approached their holy place, the sanctorum, so a church is a company of people who have been drawn together by the age-old and ever-new desire to be where God is. A company drawn together to see and hear and feel God who appeared in a man, not in the preacher, not in the deacon or elder, but God appearing in that man, back from the dead eternally alive.

That is the burning bush before which we kneel. That is the mercy seat to which we approach. That is the presence. And remember that God is literally present though not physically present. It is a mistake to imagine that He is physically present. The Bible teaches us not that He is physically present, but that He is literally present, and this then is the bush. God was not physically present in the burning bush. He was not physically present between the wings of the cherubim.

He was not physically present in the cloud and fire. But in all three He was literally present.

Let us have faith to discern the presence that is the body, of which He is the head, and that this is the holy place—after the manner of the holy place of the Old Testament temple—and let us forgive each other as God has for Christ's sake forgiven us. Will you look in your own heart and see if there is a grudge you hold against anyone? You say, yes there is, but that person has never repented. You must not wait till that person repents but rather forgive now without waiting for that person to repent. Then we must vow obedience before our God. We must put away this scattering of our attention.

If you could have a sense of His presence, it would change your life from this moment on, as long as you live. It would be like giving a weak, tired, sick man an injection of the elixir of life. It would change you so completely, elevate, purify and deliver you from the crumbles of carnal flesh to a point where your life would be one radiant fascination from this hour on.

What is important is that a company of believers is drawn by fascination to the person of God to the focal point where His presence is manifested. The best we know how to do is celebrate His death till He returns, and we can say, "If there's any irreverent thought, if there is an unforgiving thought, if there's a disobedient heart, I can only pray God to have mercy on them for they know not what they do." That we would discern the body and acknowledge the bush.

Fascination goes back into the biblical doctrine of the divine image, that we are made in the image of God and that which was made in the image of another has a desire to look in on and see that other in whose image it was made. This is the fascination, the longing to find God. But because man has sinned, he is also afraid of God, and so like Adam flees among the trees of the garden.

Some, particularly the Greeks, thought of God as dwelling in the local habitation, and so they had their sacred mount or their grove or rocky peak, and they thought of God as dwelling there. They came to worship God who dwells in the mounts or in the grove or on that rocky peak. As they approached it, the thought that God was actually there transported them, and history tells us this in some of their ecstatic songs and dances. They brought along with them heifers with garlands of flowers round their necks, and there, in front of that mount or grove or peak, they sacrificed reverently them, and the poets of the day wrote verse to their deities and sang them with the people. This was the effort of men who are lost and away from God, but who are caught in the strange fascination that God exerts over the minds of men who long to find Him but could not.

Then God brought the proof to the world and swept away errors and fancies and shadows. He showed what the Old Testament had hinted at, what it had pointed to and what it had prepared us for, that God should appear not on a mount or in a grove, but that He should appear in the form of a man and His name shall be called Emmanuel. He could say, "He that had seen me had seen the Father."

Instead of there being a holy mount, where they lead the lowing heifers, instead of there being a holy grove where the poets compose their hymns to the deities, God now dwells in the man, who is the focal point of His manifestation. As man he is that focal point of manifestation, and as God that point may be anywhere. So that's summed up like this:

"Where two or three are gathered in my name there am I in the midst of them."

It is what Moses saw in the burning bush. This is the truth as over against all of the dim ideas that were wrought out of the darkness and confusion of unregenerate minds, and God has given us a focal point where He dwells that He is everywhere. I think it is believed by Jew and Christian that God is everywhere, but there is a point of manifestation believed by Christians and that point, that focal point of manifestation, is Jesus Christ our Lord.

As God, that point may be anywhere. He that seeks the throne of grace finds that throne in every place, and so He says, "That if two of you agree on earth concerning anything that they ask, it will be done for them by My Father in heaven. For where two or three are gathered together in My name, I am there in the midst of them" (Matthew 18:19–20).

The practice of the first Christians was very simple. They met in the name of the man who they conceived and believed to be the focal point of God's manifest presence; they met in His name. That was their mount and their grove and their bush and their mercy seat and their sanctum sanctorum, their Holy place. That man was all that the Greeks have looked after and wanted, and all that the Jews had sought after happily that they might find Him. He was all that. When they met together, they met in His name, and that man died to take away the separating wall of sin and so remove the fear but still preserve the fascination.

Those early Christians were not afraid of God. They did not bring blood. That blood, they said, was already shed by the man who is also God and the God who is also man, and therefore they were not afraid of God. They still had that reverent fascination that brought them as a magnetic attraction. It brought them to God, and they could not find this God by going into the mount, for He was not in the mount. They could not find Him and satisfy their desire for His presence by going into a grove where He did not dwell. They could not satisfy themselves by going into buildings, because Paul plainly said, "God dwells not in temples made by hand." But they satisfied that by coming together in His name, and wherever they came together like this, He was there so that wherever a group of Christians met, that was their holy place. Their sacred mount was wherever Christians came up together in the name of the Lord. They said, "This man is back from the dead and though He died He's dead no longer, and though He was in the grave He's out now, and He's in full life and power forever more."

They gathered to Him knowing that He was there, not trying to persuade Him to come, but knowing that He was there and knowing that all deity was present. Hidden from sight as He was hidden once in the pillar of cloud and fire that hovered over Israel, hidden even though all deity was there. "He that has seen Me has seen the Father" and they were all with one accord in one place. While they were gathered together unto Him they became a focal point of the manifest to deity. Suddenly they were all filled with the Holy Ghost, and in the thirteenth chapter of Acts, they ministered to the Lord and prayed, and the Holy Spirit said, "Separate to Me Barnabas and Saul." In gathering together, they had no other purpose. It is wrong for Christians to meet with any other purpose than to minister to the Lord, to recognize that here is their holy mount. Here is their sacred goal. Here is their promontory peak, sticking up against the sky where the ancient Greeks used to feign that the deities dwelt.

This assembly, this gathering together is the holy mount, the holy grove, the sacred hill, a coming before the burning bush. They ministered to the Lord together, even if it might have been hidden away somewhere for fear of the Romans or the Jews. It may have been in somebody's house. It may have been in a synagogue. It may have been in a building, whether borrowed or bought. Wherever it was, it was not the building that was holy; for being God, He could be anywhere, but they together were holy as they ministered to the Lord and prayed.

The passage in First Corinthians says there was trouble in the Corinthian Church because they met without recognizing that presence, not discerning the Lord's body. They were not required to believe that the bread and wine were God, but they were required to believe that God was present wherever Christians met to serve the bread and wine. Because they did not and would not recognize this, they were in trouble. They met together for other purposes than that of finding God at that focal point of manifestation in the person of His Son. He that eats and drinks unworthily, eats and drinks damnation, the judgment is the word to himself, not discerning the presence of the Lord, not knowing that this is the Lord's body of which He is the head. He said the result of this unworthy gathering together was that some of those Christians were weak and sickly and some actually died, for we would not rightly judge ourselves. But when we are judged, we are chastened by the Lord that we should not be condemned with the world.

When they came together, they ought to have at least the reverence of a high priest of the Old Testament when he approached the sacred holy place and put blood upon the mercy seat. They didn't, though; they came in another way.

This sense of the presence wasn't in them, and so the purpose and meaning of the communion dimmed down and it was not only true there but in other churches that were described in Revelation chapters one, two, and three. In the letters to the seven churches, He said that their love had cooled, they had left their first love, and he said that their moral lives had degenerated. He said their doctrines had wavered so that they suffered from what that woman Jezebel taught them in committing spiritual fornication and eating things offered to idols. He said that they had the name to live by, but they were dead because they didn't recognize the presence and the gathering together as believers as the holy mount, the coming up to Zion's Hill, which is the Lord Jesus Christ. This had passed away from them and was why Christ appeared with eyes of flaming fire and feet like refined brass to trample, and with a two-edged sword in His mouth to slay, just before the opening of those condemnatory letters in which He had praised and blamed and pleaded for them to get right. He revealed himself as a judge and showed the two-edged sword and felt like burnished brass. There must be judgment before there can be blessing. I pray that we may be wise enough to escape the sharp edge of that sword. I pray that we may be wise enough to avoid the frightful crushing of those trampling feet. I pray that when the flaming eyes of fire look into our hearts and question why we're here, that our motive will be found pure and holy.

O Sacred Head Now Wounded

O sacred head now wounded,
With grief and shame weighed down,
Now scornfully surrounded
With thorns thine only crown . . .
How art thou pale with anguish,
With sore abuse and scorn;
How does that visage anguish,
When once was bright as morn.

—Bernard of Clairvaux (1090–1153)

CHAPTER 15

The Man Who Saw God on the Throne

In the year that King Uzziah died, I saw the Lord
sitting on a throne, high and lifted up, and the train
of His robe filled the temple.

—ISAIAH 6:1

To know You, O God, is to experience Your presence in all of its fullness. This is not based upon my holiness, but rather Your holiness that You pour into my life. Amen.

I saiah had a similar burning-bush experience as Moses. Isaiah is trying to express that which we must acknowledge is inexpressible and he is trying to utter that which cannot be uttered, which theologians say is there, and then he is trying to express what he sees that's limited.

What Isaiah saw was wholly other than and altogether different from what he ever saw before. In all our singing, praying, worshiping, preaching, and thinking we need to draw a sharp line between that which is God and that which is not God. Isaiah had been familiar with that which was not God, all that He had created, but up until this point, Isaiah had never been introduced into the presence of the uncreated. The contrast between that which is God and that which is not God, the uncreated, was such that Isaiah's language staggered under the effort to express.

It is impossible to conceive God.

We must wake up to the fact that if we could grasp God with our intellect, we would be equal to God. I will never be, can never be equal to Him, and therefore I can never grasp God with my intellect. Yet this man Isaiah tried to do it and described what he saw, but the words were clumsy and inadequate. It always turns out this way when we try to use words to express that which we are familiar with, so how much less than can we express that which is divine.

There is a difference between God revealing himself and man discovering God. He cannot by his intellect bore through to God. He could not do it in a million years. Not all the brains in the world could in one second reveal to himself the spirit of the man until the man knows God experientially. God revealed himself to Isaiah, and everything he has written here was and is true because what is written is made great by as much as God is greater than the human mind.

Isaiah says, "I saw the Lord sitting on a throne." I wish I could make this vision, at least dimly, seen by the people of the world. God sits upon the throne. Here He is, up on the throne.

We have gotten away from this view of God now. It is evidence of anthropomorphism.

I still believe God sits upon the throne. This is self-bestowed sovereignty, and I certainly believe in the sovereignty of God. I believe that God sits upon the throne overseeing all events. That is why I can sleep at night. If I thought the events of the world were in the hands of politicians, I would not sleep tonight. God sits on His throne and He determines all events. According to the purpose, which He intended in Christ Jesus before the world began, He determined all the needs and disposing of all.

Around this throne, Isaiah describes creatures about which I know very little. The seraphim, the high exalted ones, the fiery burners are only seen once in the Scriptures. I noticed with a good deal of satisfaction that they are seen close to the throne and burning with rapturous love for the God-head. Then there was the smoke that filled the temple. Then there was the antiphon chant, "Holy, holy, holy, Lord God Almighty." I have often wondered why the dear old rabbis, saints, and hymnists of old times did not come to the knowledge of the Trinity just from hearing the seraphim chant, "Holy, holy, holy."

What does the word *holy* mean? It is the Lord of host here, and it is more than an adjective saying that God is a holy God. It is a description of glory to the triune God, and I am not sure I know what it means at all, but I will give several words, which I think may come close.

Remember, you can feel your way through to God with your heart; your mind has given up and quit because God lies out yonder, infinitely transcending all these creatures.

As the old devotional writer said, "The heart is always the best theologian."

With our hearts, we may know that at least this is purity, and it is good to know that there is something left to think about that's pure. You have to discount the world. The world says a man is always good and a woman is always good, "except." Abraham, David, and all the rest with their weaknesses and flaws. James said something about how Elijah was a man of like passions (see James 5:17). That sounds like a little bit of excusing. Elijah was a man of like passions, but it is a comforting thing to know that he was a good man and used by God, yet he was not a perfect man. That is why I feel more comfortable with Esau than I would with Joseph and Paul, who were good men with nothing written against them.

The reason we do not have more repentance is that we repent for what we do instead of what we are. Remember, repentance for what you do goes deep, but what you are goes deeper. Plus, if you go deeper, it is a sharp contrast between what God is and what Isaiah was, the absolute holiness of the deity in the spotted, speckled impurities of Isaiah's nature brought absolute proof to this man of God.

Then there is mystery. This always baffles and stuns the mind. We come before God in speechless humility, in the presence of the inexpressible. I feel that we should always leave room for mystery in our Christian faith. When we do not, we become evangelical rationalists and can explain everything. Just ask any question and we are quick and eager to answer that question. But I do not believe we really can. I think there is mystery running throughout all the kingdom of God. Just as there is mystery running throughout all of the kingdom of nature.

The honest scientist is open to learning more. He realizes he doesn't know everything. So, too, a Christian needs to allow an open mind when it comes to fellowship with someone who doesn't believe *exactly* as he believes.

When I hear a man pray too fluently, I know he has not seen anything because of his ability to express himself in prayer, unless he should experience a sudden passionate outpouring of the Holy Ghost upon him, but with just an average man, when we are praying too fluently we're not seeing much.

Then there was strangeness, like nothing we know, remote and unknown. What we try to do in our terrible day is to control God, think Him down where we can use Him, and we even believe in somebody up there who likes us.

The manifest presence of God is something different. It is beyond us. It is above us. It is transcendent and we cannot get through to it on our own. We have to throw our hearts open and say, "God, shine on my understanding." Otherwise, we will not see God on His throne. It is something portentous, dreadful, and terrifying. Isaiah writes later, "Who among us shall dwell with the devouring fire? Who among us shall dwell with everlasting burnings?" (Isaiah 33:14).

The everlasting fire, the eternal burning, is God who is a consuming fire. It is a fatal thing to fall in the hands of this living God. Isaiah saw the heavens opened and fire coming out. He saw the four-faced creature out of the fire. As Christians, we should be men and women out of the fire.

The Christian should never be the kind of person that can be explained.

God is holy, He is actively hostile to sin, and He must be. Only God can burn on and on forever. Never let any spiritual experience or any interpretation of Scripture trim your hatred for sin. Even if you fall into it yourself, hate it with a holy hatred and get out of that sin. Sin brought the downfall of the race. Sin brought the Savior to die on the Roman cross. Sin has filled every jail. Sin is silent; it is sin that has motivated every murder and every divorce and every crime committed since the world began. In the presence of this awful, holy God, sin can never be anything but heinous deformity.

The man of God, Isaiah, had a vision here and was seeing something that was there.

He saw God and if we open our eyes, we would see God. God is everywhere.

I am afraid, unconsciously, that many will say, "I can do it." No, my brother, you cannot do it. There are no institutions of learning in the world where you could go through them all and learn everything that can be learned and read what they wrote. There is not enough knowledge in the world to enable you to do the job the Holy Ghost is sending you out to do. He will use your instruments, your skills, your gifts. I believe in that, all right. He will never allow you to do it by yourself. You must be undone.

The man God uses is the man that has been undone. The man who sees God sitting upon a throne is undone. Here is an astonished man whose whole world suddenly dissolves into vast, eternal darkness, and he was against it, red and black. He said, "Mine eyes have seen the King."

What kind of man was Isaiah anyhow? Was he a murderer, a liar, or a drunkard? No, he was a fine young, cultured fellow, cousin of the king, poet in his own right. Isaiah was a good man and could have been elected to any mission board or anything else. I wish I, by nature, were half as good. After all, what is man over against the eternal likeness? What is the purest morality over against the holiness of the unspeakable holy God? Isaiah, when he cried out, "I am undone," meant that what he was experiencing was more than being undone over against the holiness of the creator, so that what we hear in his words, "I am undone," is the cry of pain.

This is why I do not like the kind of evangelism that sugarcoats everything. I believe there ought to be a cry of pain. I think there ought to be a birth from within. I fear that there should be a terror of seeing ourselves in violent contrast to the holy, holy, holy God. Unless we do, our repentance will never go deep, and if our repentance does not go deep, our Christian experience will not go deep. Here was a man who was crying out, not because of what he had done, for he did not mention a single sin.

It is not the question of whether we have Isaiah's uncleanness or not, but whether we have his awareness. He was unclean and, thank God, he became aware of it. The world today is unclean but unaware of it. The uncleanness without awareness, without terrible consequences, is what is wrong with the world, and that is what is wrong with the church and what is wrong with Christians today. We are unclean without being aware. Uncleanness without awareness makes us very bold and self-assured, gives us a sense of our own holiness and creates false assurance.

When we see God on the throne in the eyes of our heart, and utilizing the theology the Bible gives us, we mount by faith and by inward illumination to behold a little of how holy God is. After that, there will never be depravity. I have always believed in the depravity of man. John Calvin did not invent that; David talked about that long before Calvin. The first baby born was born depraved.

But you say, of course, they are depraved, the harlots and publicans. But you know, that is not our problem. Our problem is the depravity in the circle of the just, among the saints, among those who claim to be great souls and whose pictures get in the papers and who have things named after them.

Isaiah knew he was bad, but now he had a sense of moral innocence, and it is all the wonder of God's grace that we can know how bad we are too. Likewise, after we have gone through this humiliating experience ourselves and the coals of fire touched our lips, the past with its deep iniquity, we can acknowledge how bad we are. Not our sins committed, but our sins uncommitted, and His grace touches us, and we have that sense of restored moral innocence, the forgiving love of God. Then God said what He had said before, "Who shall I send, and who will go for us?" Then Isaiah said, "Here am I, send me."

This was a man God could use. A man whose integrity was taken away. Let us never take anything for granted. You know the one that I pray for the most in my pastoral work, the one that gives me the most trouble, is myself.

After this purifying experience for Isaiah, then God says, I will use you. So He sent Isaiah out.

Hallelujah, Praise Jehovah

Let them praises give Jehovah,
They were made at His command;
Them forever He established,
His decree shall ever stand,
From the earth, O praise Jehovah,
All ye floods, ye dragons all,
Fire and hail and snow and vapors,
Stormy winds that hear Him call.

—William J. Kirkpatrick (1838–1921)

CHAPTER 16

Creatures Out of the Fire

As for the likeness of their faces, each had the face of a man; each of the four had the face of a lion on the right side, each of the four had the face of an ox on the left side, and each of the four had the face of an eagle.

—EZEKIEL 1:10

O God and Father of our Lord Jesus Christ, it is in the fire that I see the beauty of Christ and His application to my life. Praise You for who He is, and praise You that He is in me. Amen.

E zekiel 1:10 starts with, "As for the likeness of their faces," and goes on with how they had the face of a man, a lion, an ox, an eagle.

Long before I knew this verse applied to the Lord Jesus Christ and the gospel, I perceived it was saying that the four Gospels were the figures of a man over Luke; a lion over Matthew; an ox over Mark; and an eagle over John.

But these living creatures—described later as cherub in Ezekiel 10:4—that Ezekiel saw in his vision do indeed describe one figure: Jesus Christ—the center of creation to whom God directs all our eyes. For the Lord said, "Behold! My Servant . . . in whom My soul delights" (Isaiah 42:1).

All of creation exists to show Jesus Christ for us. Still, not all of creation can set forth the glory of Christ, for Christ is the glory of God and creation is the glory of Christ. These creatures reveal Christ's attraction. Not all His attractions can be put together in one face.

If everything that He has done was written down, the world could not contain the books. It would take not only this creation, which men have called the universe, but it would take a dozen other universes to show forth the wonders and the glory that belongs to Jesus Christ.

Our goal is to be like Christ. The hymn's refrain, "Oh, to be like Thee, Oh, to be like Thee," sums up the yearning of the heart of a Christian. This is not simply a sentimental yearning, but a sound theological fact with sound biblical reason behind it.

God made His Son to be a man and sent Him among us, and He made us to be like His Son. First God made man in His own image. When man sinned, God made His Son in the likeness of man, barring sin, and now He is making man again in the likeness of His Son. So when we look at anything that sets forth the glory of Jesus Christ our Lord, we look at the model of what we should be.

Christ did not apologize when He came into the world to be incarnated. He did not go as society goes to the slums, careful and timid. But He came down, as far as it was possible to go, and went through the simple and blunt process of being born of a virgin mother. Thus, He became a man and took upon himself our humanity.

Christ thus assumed the exalted work of human nature and stayed in character. Christ was the only perfect example of an unsoiled human being.

We know very little about Adam and Eve before the fall— that happy, blissful period when they dwelt in their unabashed nakedness in the presence of God and each other, their own humility their only covering. However, we know a great deal about them afterward, after they sinned and God drove them out of the garden. The Bible tells us about Adam and Eve and all their descendants, including ourselves, sad and disappointing as we are. When our Lord Jesus Christ came to the world, He had the simple weakness of man, but not the weakness of sin. He could become tired and need to rest and sleep and eat, but that was His humanity. That was not fallen humanity. Christ did not take upon himself fallen humanity.

If you want to see humanity at its most delightful, perfect stage, look at Jesus Christ, our Lord. He never tried to be anything He was not, and He had nothing to hide. There was no perversion in Him. Christ was humanity walking upright without perversion, without affectation, without pride and fear.

These are the devils that work on humanity: perversion, affectation, pride, and fear. They seek to destroy us like insects in a garden. There we grow, but the fruit we bear is poor, wormy, shrunken, undersized fruit.

When the simple beauty of Jesus' humanity was lost under the leaves of tradition, men went away and hid themselves, trying to be good. They said the only way to be good is to get away from people. You'll get tainted by contact, they said. But a lily can grow out of a manure pile, out in the farmyard, and be unsullied and pure, growing in the sunshine, fragrant and beautiful, untouched by the very soil it grows in and its surroundings.

So it was with Jesus. Our Lord was no ascetic. He walked among wicked, vicious, evil, proud, and hypocritical men. Unlike John the Baptist, who came not eating and drinking, Jesus came eating and drinking. He went among the people simply. He did not believe He could make His soul good by punishing His stomach, and He did not believe that by not eating He could become a good man. He knew better.

Our Lord had absolutely nothing of that. God made the human body to be a temple of the Holy Ghost, and He does not punish His temple.

Our Lord was not a hater of people. Many good people have withdrawn themselves in cold scorn of the human race that our Lord was friendly to. He dwelt among sinners as holy and undefiled and higher than the heavens, and yet He loved people.

We are going to be redeemed men and women in heaven. Nothing higher is possible for us. So, to be redeemed humans, cleansed now and purified and Spirit-filled, that is the ideal. Because in doing so, we would be like Jesus Christ our Lord.

The Face of the Lion

Lions are admired for their courage, dignity, confidence, poise, and daring. Have you ever been at a zoo and seen a great bearded lion? They look out at you there. They cross their great paws and never quite look at you; so dignified, always looking past you. They always look just a little to your right or left, but never right at you, as if you amount to absolutely nothing. "You see me? I am the king of the jungle!" I imagine them thinking. Again, there is something about the dignity and courage and poise of the lion.

These qualities were large in Jesus Christ. They were part of His perfect humanity. He didn't cringe and apologize. He went about as a man among men, with no timidity, no shrinking.

We are told to be humble, but don't be any humbler than you need to be. God never said to us, "Be thou a mouse." He simply said, "Humble yourselves under the mighty hand of God" (1 Peter 5:6). What he meant was, come down to your size. I like to have people be like a lion and be courageous; be what they are.

We Christians have gone off the attack and we're on the defense. You never see a lion on the defensive. We need to be

Spirit-filled, praying, courageous, poised, and self-assured in the right sense of the word, not trusting in self but trusting in the God within us, the face of the lion.

The Face of an Ox

There is something in Christ's character that only the ox, as they knew it in Bible times and down the years, sets forth properly. What is this that an ox has that a lion doesn't have? What is this that an ox has that an eagle doesn't have? It took all of the creatures in Ezekiel's vision to reveal Christ's glory.

An ox has shortcomings. I date back to a time when I saw oxen hitched up and with yokes on their necks, pulling things. They do not have grace. That's sure enough. And they don't have much for brains. Nor do they have charm.

But here is what an ox has: patience, steadfastness, calm perseverance, and resignation. I have never seen an excited ox or one in a big hurry. The ox is always patient and steadfast. And this is what our Lord had when He lived among men. He endured everything patiently and quietly.

The Face of the Eagle

The four creatures in Ezekiel's vision of God don't contradict each other, they complement each other. They fill out each other, and by looking at the four pictures, we see a little more of what Christ was like and what we ought to be like characteristically.

We see Jesus Christ our Lord walking as calmly and as steadfastly among men as the plodding ox, walking with all the courage and poise of the lion, walking with a simple, relaxed dignity of a man. Yet there was an area in the life of Christ far out of sight. There was an area in the character and nature of Christ that never touched the earth at all, that roamed higher in the sun until the eagle got here to reveal another side of the character of Jesus Christ, our Lord. Look at the characteristics of the eagle, his aspiration, attitude, the high peaks, the sunshine, and the wingspread.

He who was among men said the son of man who is in the bosom of the Father left and when He was walking on earth clearly said, "He is in the bosom of the Father." And He said, "I know Thou hears me always." Jesus Christ never left the Father's bosom when He came to the womb of the virgin. Something in His nature still held tight and was in touch with all the infinite power that is God. And He never allowed himself to settle down into the dust, though He walked among men and got dust on His holy feet; still, like the eagle He soared out of sight.

And it is said of us that we shall mount up with wings as eagles. God means for His children to live another kind of life. There should be overtones of heaven upon the Christian heart always. Now, Christ our Lord lived like that. But we are too much contented with visible things. Too much contented with visible services. If we are in touch with God when we come to church, we would find our services stepped up by several hundred percent in one day. But only a few are in touch with God, maybe, and the rest are loosely in touch with God, and some not at all. And the result is that the total climate of the service is not very beautiful because there are so few that have come in touch with God.

As Christians, we ought to try to be holy men and women— not ashamed of our humanity but grateful for it. I wouldn't trade being a human being for anything in the world. I would rather be a redeemed man than a seraphim. I would rather be a redeemed man than a lion, ox, or eagle because these creatures are only there to set forth Christ. You and I can have Christ's holy and beautiful characteristics, which far transcend that of any other creatures.

So, the Christian dwelt in the secret place and he sees everything from the heights. It is amazing how much better things look from upstairs. And when you look down on anything, it is wonderful how much better it looks. The birds that soar and circle have a different view of the world than men who tread along on the road, or the ox, for that matter. But it takes both. An eagle that soars yonder could never plow a furrow, and if Christ had lived only in the high peaks, He never could have walked among men and allowed His hand to be tied in front of Him and finally to be nailed to the cross, never. He had to come down and live the patient life of the ox among men. If He had had only the high-flying characteristics of the eagle, He never could have faced up to Judas and Peter and Pilate and Herod and the rest of them. But because He had the courage of a lion, He stood and calmly took it.

But if He had only had the characteristics of the faithful ox, He never could have said, "But I see, I speak unto you," the son of man which came down from heaven. I utter the things which I have seen, and I say to you these things. You do not understand because you are of the earth, earthly, with too much earth in you; too much earth in you. But there's something else in you too, that is the mystical side, the spiritual side. This high-flying side is filled with aspiration and yearning after the things of God.

Hear the Lord of Harvest Sweetly Calling

When the coal of fire touched the prophet,
Making him as pure, as pure can be,
When the voice of God said, "Who'll go for us?"
Then he answered, "Here I am, send me."

—George Bennard (1873–1958)

CHAPTER 17

The God Who Manifests Himself

And it came to pass after many days that the word of the LORD came to Elijah, in the third year, saying, "Go, present yourself to Ahab, and I will send rain on the earth."

—1 KINGS 18:1

O Father, I delight in Your presence in my life. How thankful I am that You show yourself to me and cause me to trust in You. I praise You, that You are not an absentee presence. Amen.

This God of Elijah is a God who manifests himself. I want you to notice here that God manifested himself to Elijah and the people under Elijah's direction. And the Lord God was tapping on the window all the time trying to get through and manifest himself. He manifested himself in fire, sure, but He also manifested himself in a still, small voice and providence and prayer. God is ready to make himself known. Manifest means to show himself. He's ready to take the veil away from himself and shine through upon His church. He's the God who manifests himself, and He is the God who works the miracles.

I believe this with all my heart. I'm not a miracle monger and do not believe we ever ought to announce, "We're going to have a miracle night." God works miracles, but you cannot tell God what to do. If you have faith, then in humility you can trust something is divinely caused, an event in nature that does not have natural causes. An event that while not contrary to nature, nevertheless rises above nature, because the source is in God. And God does miracles.

Look at the widow's oil and meal and how God kept that thing going. He kept one little cruise of oil and one little barrel of meal going for a whole year or two, while she fed her family and a strange man of God that had come to them. And then when the boy died, Elijah raised him from the dead.

Remember when Elijah was in great straits the Lord said to him, "Elijah, go down to the brook and I'll cause the water of the brook to flow by and you drink of the brook." And He said, "I'll cause the ravens to bring you meat."

Later on, when the brook dried up Elijah said, "There'll be no rain." But he forgot if there's no rain, there'll be no brook. So later when it did not rain, the brook dried up and Elijah was in an awful situation. He took his little cup one morning and started for the water. When he got down there all he saw was a red lizard looking out on a perfectly dry, sandy bottom of the little brook. Elijah said, "My God, the water's gone." And God said, "What did you expect? You said there would be no rain, so no rain, no brook. But I've taken care of it." And God sent him over to Zarephath, to a widow. She said to Elijah, "We're going to eat this and after that nothing, we'll die."

Elijah said, "No. I'm serving God and He told me that if you look after me, He'll take care of you." And for two or three years, He did.

Remember those cakes the angel made for Elijah? I've been delighted with this because here was Elijah now when he'd lost his courage temporarily. He had courage, he was a very courageous man, but that woman Jezebel, she must have been a terror. Because when she sent word, he lit out. He wasn't afraid of her husband. "I stand before the Lord." But when Jezebel started for him, Elijah forgot that he'd stood before the Lord and so he started for the mountains. And he was going to hole up where it was safe, and the Lord said to an angel, "Now, Elijah, he's down there and he's in bad shape. He's under a juniper tree and he's lost heart and he's discouraged and blue and frightened and wants to die.

He's my servant and he loves me and he has faith and I can't overlook him. You go bake him some cakes." God sent an angel to bake cakes for a prophet. Oh, God is a very tender, loving God, and we ought to keep that in mind.

That is who the Lord God of Elijah is. He's God the Father Almighty, who manifests himself to His people, either inwardly or by miracles and whirlwinds. One way or another, that's the way God does it.

Now, where is the Lord God of Elijah? And I'd like to say the Lord God of Elijah is near. He's very near; He's here now and He's here now waiting for certain ones of us, men and women, to meet certain conditions.

Let me name them for you.

God is here today as He was there then, and there is nothing to prevent us from seeing God do anything now that He did then, when it is needed to be done. The Lord God of Elijah is here waiting for somebody as fearless as Elijah was. Elijah was a fearless man, though he admits that he had that one little breakdown there.

That woman Jezebel came for him and he lit out. Apart from that, he was a fearless man of great courage. There's danger today and it takes courage to have that Mount Carmel experience. It takes a lot of courage to stand out. Trying to get along with each other so that you never have any trouble and never get in trouble always weakens us. There were several men, there were men of God, there was this prophet, Obadiah, and He had hundreds of prophets hidden in a cave.

Imagine being hidden in a cave when Jezebel was on the loose with Ahab, the wickedest king that had been since Jeroboam. Here were men hiding away in a cave and only one had the courage to go up and down into the country, and that was Elijah. If all those two hundred prophets, each in his own right, had on him the spirit of Elijah, they'd have shaken Israel to her foundation. They would've frightened Jezebel back to Sidon where she belonged, and Ahab would've crawled in a hole somewhere and pulled it in after him; the power of God would've leaped out on Israel. But here they were hiding; it takes some courage.

Elijah had courage, and we always have had men of courage down through the years; it takes a lot of courage to stand for God in an hour like this. To stand for God among men; to be a son of God among the sons of men; to be a citizen of heaven among the citizens of the earth and to be a good man in a bad world. To have faith in a world of unbelief and to want to be good in a world that loves to be bad; it takes courage. All God is waiting on is for men and women to rise with something of the fearlessness of the man Elijah, with his same consecration. I know it may sound commonplace, but Elijah was a consecrated man. They use the word *dedicated* now; they say, "He's a dedicated man," and by that they mean he's dedicated to politics or science or something else. But we believe that dedication ought to be to God and completely dedicated to Him, consecrated.

Then there is being as obedient as Elijah was. You notice that Elijah was an obedient man. It says here that he went and did according to the word of the Lord. Every time God spoke to him, he went and did according to the word of the Lord. And because he went and did according to the word of the Lord, God did according to the word of Elijah, and the two of them worked together on things. God said, "Elijah, do this," and Elijah ran and did it, and Elijah said, "Oh God, do this," and God ran and did it. God and Elijah worked together because Elijah listened to the word of the Lord; the Lord listened to the word of Elijah.

God's looking for obedient people. Obedient, I mean positively obedient, not just passively obedient.

Christ's church today is cursed with passive obedience, which is, of course, actually disobedience. We sing, "Have thine own way, have thine own way" and never do a thing. You have to be obedient. If the Lord wants you to give a certain amount of money, write a check. Don't hug your checkbook to your chest and sing, "Have thine own way, Lord"; write your check. If God wants you to go to a prayer meeting, don't put on your slippers and sing, "Have thine own way"; go to the prayer meeting. If it is raining, go anyhow. God is waiting for somebody as obedient as Elijah was.

I believe God is finding people as full of faith as Elijah, a sink-or-swim kind of faith. Many people have the kind of faith Martha had. She said, "Yes, I know, Lord. He'll arise in the last day." And the Lord said, "That's not the kind of faith that works. I want you to believe he'll rise now; right *now*."

While looking for the rose-bordered path, Elijah took the tough, vital way of faith and obedience. He put himself, as they say, on the spot. That takes a hazardous faith, and we have to have it.

Lastly, God is looking for somebody as prayerful as Elijah. Elijah prayed and he prayed again. He lived for prayer, he commanded in prayer, and he made claims from prayer. We sit down and say, "Where's the Lord God of Elijah," as we mournfully sing, "Where are the Good Old Days?"

No, we don't want the good old days. Rather, we want the God of the good old days.

Electrical outlets are 120 volts. The power surging in them is very quiet, but still, there's power there that will work your vacuum cleaner, keep your radio on, cook your meals, let you shave with it, and run your power mower . . . it's all there. But it has to have a condition met: You must plug in to the source, and then that power hums away.

God Almighty is here, not far away. Still, people say, "I don't hear Him." Of course they don't. I don't hear Him either, but He's here. How do I know? I know, because if I meet the conditions, I get the power. Just like electricity, you can't hear it or see it, but it is there because the lights are working.

Elijah's God is our God today—the God and Father of Jesus Christ. He is a God who works miracles, but there must be conditions met: faith and obedience. Plug them in to the mighty source and you'll have the power that Elijah had. The Lord God of Elijah is here waiting, waiting for a fearless people and a consecrated people and obedient people and faith-filled, prayerful people. And when He finds them, He will begin to do for them what He did for people in other days.

Let us then rise and dare to say, "O Lord God, help us." Let us stop talking about yesterday and begin talking about the possibilities of our tomorrows.

Faith of Our Fathers

Faith of our fathers, living still
In spite of dungeon, fire and sword,
O how our hearts beat high with joy
Whene'er we hear that glorious word!
Faith of our fathers! Holy faith!
We will be true to Thee till death!

—Frederick W. Faber (1814–1863) /
Henri F. Hemy (1818–1888)

CHAPTER 18

Elijah and the Fire

And Elijah came to all the people, and said, "How long will you falter between two opinions? If the Lord is God, follow Him; but if Baal, follow him." But the people answered him not a word.

—1 KINGS 18:21

Father, we pray that the Spirit of God, Your Spirit, the Spirit of the Father and the Son, may take this ancient truth and let it be released in power tonight over our consciences. Lord, we haven't long and we're in great need, so we beseech You, O risen Lord Jesus, confirm Your word. Confirm Your word and perform a council of Your messengers. Amen.

This chapter covers a low period in Israel's history when the nation should have been committed to the highest righteousness in personal living and conduct and the purest worship of the Most High God. In spite of God's covenant and His giving of the law and privileges, their lives demonstrated a continual and constant controversy going on between them and God. The chief blame belonged to someone I call the Sidonian vampire, Jezebel.

Jezebel was the wife of Ahab, the king of Israel. He wasn't much of a king, really, but he filled the place for a time. His wife was not Jewish. She was the daughter of the king of Sidon, and thus she was a Sidonian and a Baalite, someone who worshiped Baal. Ahab was a Jew and was supposed to be a worshiper of Jehovah, the great God, the I Am, *that* I Am. Even though the Baalites were set against the Most High God, Ahab apparently wanted a wife from the royal family of Sidon, so he picked this good-looking Jezebel and married her.

The worship of Baal involved cruel and immoral rituals. And Jezebel was the evangelist of the hour. Not for Jehovah or decency and righteousness, but for Baal and evil.

All this led to a moral dilemma for Israel. Here was the royal family, a Hebrew with his wife, a Sidonian. The king was committed, at least nominally, to the worship of Jehovah, and his queen was committed positively to the worship of Baal.

This reminds me of a passage of Scripture that is very mysterious. There's much to say about it, though I must say it may lead to being accused of being a mystic. The verse (John 1:9) says Christ was the true Light, giving light to every man that comes into the world. So even the man or woman who has never heard of the Bible, God, or the gospel, nor anything having to do with revealed religion, still has more light than we imagine. For every person has been, in some measure, illuminated by "the true Light" so that they know something of what is right and wrong.

If you're worrying about crooked politicians and movie actresses with five husbands, change it around and thank God for the good people you know. Sometime when you're feeling real mean, when you just feel emotional as if you were not a Christian at all, your faith is holding and you really do know who you are. Your anchor holds in the storms of life, but if there are times when nothing seems right, get down on your knees and then on a piece of paper write down the names of the good people you know. Be grateful to God for the ability to appreciate them.

Israel should have known right and wrong by the deep wisdom that lights up every man. God's people also had access to divine revelation, the Holy Scriptures, which nobody else had. Even though they should have known what was right, who to worship, how they should live, Jezebel set the standard for morality and worship. However she chose to dress and live, others followed her ways. They also worshiped the way she worshiped, because the people were too weak and cowardly to obey God, and they found it easier to follow what was in vogue. That's always the easiest thing.

If you're going to be a Christian, you're going to have to learn to stand against what's in vogue. You're going to have to learn to listen to the voice of God and heed the sound of an inaudible drum. There are people marching all together in another parade, and a world marching to the world's music is going the wrong direction.

We're going to have to decide whether this religion business is of God, whether God's in this, whether the Bible is real, whether hell is hell and heaven is heaven, or whether we can just follow what's in vogue and be like everybody else. You're going to have to make up your mind.

As I said, Israel was in a dilemma, and, of course, nobody's at rest when they're in that condition because deep down people know when they are following a band or parade that isn't going to heaven. They know they're being cheated, robbed of something very precious, and it worries them. A man knows he's dishonoring his soul, and he's deeply ashamed until he covers it up with amusements. He knows he's violating the holy laws of God and it makes him afraid, but of course, the effect will depend upon the degree of light.

Will we worship Baal or Jehovah? If Baal, 1 Kings 18:21 applies: "How long will you falter between two opinions?"

I say the religion of our day is the religion of Baal. It is a religion that will let you get away with anything, if you just talk about love and the unity of mankind and the brotherhood of the world. If you just talk nice and sound pious, you can do just about anything; the sky's the limit. And there's no morality, no righteousness, no godliness required, just live any way you want, provided that in the end you say, "Well, we're all going the same way, we're just going by different roads." It sounds so very spiritual, but it's just the way the Baalite lady Jezebel talked.

She told them, "Now, you Jews, don't you know that Baal has something to be said in his favor too." Of course! They have sex orgies and rites of iniquity to worship him, but that's all right. That's our way of looking at things.

What does Baal offer? What does the chief shallow religious world offer? They offer a few things. They offer the customary fun and conformity. If you do it, if you conform and go along with the crowd, they had to have it. But Jehovah, He called you to the good, hard way; the good, hard way with its present cost and its eternal compensation. What has Baal to offer? What has the world to offer? Will we surrender to the world? What has it really to offer? It would lead you to think it has a great deal to offer, but how utterly helpless it is when tragedy strikes.

A trimmed-down gospel never saved a soul. A trimmed-down, diluted, edited religion is not the religion that Christ died to establish. And the heaven over yonder is not filled full of weaklings who had to have somebody to go along and help them over the rough spots. It is full of people—soldiers and the martyr and the dreamer and the prophet and the rule followers—who loved God and loved their generation and lived and died having lived a good life, a hard life. We've got to make up our minds. Are we going to go the way the world goes? Jezebel will see to that. What are we going to do about it?

Baal has a lot to offer; we might as well admit it. I've heard the preachers talk about how burdened down men are with sin, picturing them with great weights on their backs, and preachers say there's no pleasure in sin. Of course sin has pleasure, but you've got to break with it and follow Jehovah. The worse the country is, the worse the state of society, the harder it is to break and the more it is going to cost you to break from sin's pleasure.

Make up your mind. Don't be in the middle because you're neither hot nor cold. God will spew you out of His mouth. The only place in the Bible where God gets sick is when He faces up to people who can't make up their mind about whether to serve God or Baal. I believe that God has more respect for a Baalite down on his knees before a sex altar than He does for the fellow caught in the middle who is afraid to worship God, trembling in the middle between right and wrong.

Does that describe you? God says it makes Him sick, and He spews you out of His mouth.

If Jehovah is God and Jesus Christ did indeed say, "Come and take up your cross and follow me," there will be a judgment. God is to judge every person's heart according to their thoughts and according to their deeds. With Baal, you've had your fun, but the day is coming to take your medicine. Every time you're led astray, remember the person that leads you astray really leaves you in the lurch.

When Judas Iscariot betrayed Christ, Judas was deserted by the people to whom he had sold Christ. With a spasm of conscience, Judas went back to the priests and said, "Here, take the money." But they turned coldly away and said, "What is that to us?" It's always like that—people will lead you astray and then leave you in the end.

But thank God for the one named Jesus, who leads us on the right path and never leaves us.

The Baalites had their fun, but they couldn't be cleansed inside. You're going to die someday, and I trust you want to die with a clean conscience. How do you do that? The blood of Jesus Christ cleanses you from all sin. So if Baal is your god, serve him, but he'll never forgive your sins, never cleanse you within. Want somebody who can direct you and lead you through that cleansing process? Baal can't do it. Baal can have a big-time Saturday night, but he will leave you with a frightful hangover Sunday morning. Baal just can't help you through in the end.

I always pray and look to God. Sometimes I've blundered, but I keep going to Him. I do not run around asking advice from people who don't know any more about Him than I do. The Scriptures say God's name shall be Counselor. Jesus Christ, the Lord, leads the blind by the way they don't know. He guides them in paths where they have not been. He makes the darkness light before them, when they can't think straight. He does all this.

If you choose Baal, if you choose anything other than the true God, you go without a counselor, an advocate. If you choose Baal, you go without anybody to direct your way. If you choose the world, you go without cleansing and forgiveness.

Then there's the hereafter. I like to think about the hereafter. Of course, we want something in the by-and-by. It is a complete fool who lives his life out to the end not knowing what's out there. I want to know what's out there.

Good people live in expectation of the world to come. Nobody's going to shame me because I believe in God, the Father Almighty. I also believe in His Son, Jesus Christ our Lord, and I believe in the Holy Ghost and the forgiveness of sin and life everlasting.

But Baal doesn't have it. The world out there doesn't have it. That slick world that comes into your home by TV doesn't have it. And that theater doesn't have it. They don't have it out there, brother. Only Jesus has it. "No one comes to the Father except through Me."

So, if you want forgiveness of sin, inward cleansing, the power to direct your life and the advocate God for you above, a counselor to take you through, peace at last, and a place in the Father's house, I recommend Jesus Christ, now.

Our story in 1 Kings 18 ends with the Baalites calling out to their god, but no answer came. They prayed all day and cut themselves all day, but still nothing happened. Then Elijah prayed to the Most High God, and in no time, fire came down. God confirmed Elijah's faith and gave witness to his obedience. And that's what God will do for you.

Guide Me, O Thou Great Jehovah

Open now the crystal fountain,
Whence the healing stream doth flow;
Let the fire and cloudy pillar
Lead me all my journey through.
Strong Deliverer, strong Deliverer,
Be Thou still my Strength and Shield.

—William Williams (1717–1791) /
Harry E. Fosdick (1878–1969) /
John Hughes (1873–1932) /
Peter Williams (1722–1796)

CHAPTER 19

Fire in the Furnace

Then King Nebuchadnezzar was astonished; and he
rose in haste and spoke, saying to his counselors,
"Did we not cast three men bound into the midst
of the fire?" They answered and said to the king,
"True, O king." "Look!" he answered, "I see four
men loose, walking in the midst of the fire; and
they are not hurt, and the form of the fourth is like
the Son of God."

—DANIEL 3:24–25

*I thank You, O Father, for the fiery furnaces that You have
established in my life. It is in these furnaces that I truly experience Your presence that separates me from the world around
me. Praise Your name, amen.*

When Moses encountered the fire in the bush, he was meeting God for the very first time. It was his first experience in the presence of God. Notwithstanding, this experience changed Moses for the rest of his life.

That change in Moses brought him to the place where he could be used by God to rescue His people.

Many years later we come to the story of Shadrach, Meshach, and Abed-Nego. These three were acquainted with God and companions of Daniel, even though in bondage to Babylon. King Nebuchadnezzar had authority over their life, or so he thought.

The enemies of God and Daniel and these three young men were trying to get rid of them because of their rising popularity, as far as Nebuchadnezzar was concerned. They knew how devoted these young men were to God, and that was how they were going to bring their downfall.

In Daniel 3:10–11, we read that whoever did not bow down and worship Nebuchadnezzar, their god, would be cast into the midst of a burning fiery furnace. Nebuchadnezzar bought into this plan because it made him important, but what he did not know was there would be some people that would refuse to bow to this god.

These young men were brought before Nebuchadnezzar, who tried to persuade them to go along with the culture of the time.

That is what is happening today. The Nebuchadnezzars around us want the church to go along with the culture so as not to upset anybody. These young men put God first and would not allow anything to move them away from that priority, not even death.

On several occasions, Nebuchadnezzar tried to convince them that it would be all right. "Yes, you can serve your God, but would you just, for my sake, bow down and worship this idol?" More of a business transaction than anything else, so what is the harm?

He thought he could convince them, but he did not understand their commitment to God, which was more important to them than even life itself.

Nebuchadnezzar threatened if they did not do this, he would throw them into a fiery furnace, and they would die.

I am sure Shadrach, Meshach, and Abed-Nego were frightened of the fiery furnace. But their commitment to God outweighed their fear of the fiery furnace and their loyalty to King Nebuchadnezzar.

Verses 17 and 18 of Daniel chapter three are important for us: "Our God whom we serve is able to deliver us from the burning fiery furnace, and He will deliver us from your hand, O king. But if not, let it be known to you, O king, that we do not serve your gods, nor will we worship the gold image which you have set up."

It finally came to the point where Nebuchadnezzar, to protect his reputation, had to have these three young men cast into the fiery furnace. I am sure he did not want to do this because he respected these people for their wisdom and how they were a blessing to Babylon at the time.

The interesting thing here is, the fire killed the men who bound up these three and cast them into the furnace, but the young men were not killed.

It seems to me what God is saying here is that if we put our trust in Him, He will destroy our enemy. Our enemy is trying to destroy us. But in reality, that enemy is putting us in a place where we can experience God as we have never experienced Him before.

Because of Nebuchadnezzar's anger at the time, he heated the furnace seven times hotter than normal. This, of course, killed the men who were throwing these young men into the flame. Inside the furnace, the bonds on their hands and legs were burnt, but the fire did not touch them.

When Nebuchadnezzar looked into the fire, he was astonished to see not three but four men walking in the midst of the fire; and the form of the fourth was like the Son of God. Indeed, in this fiery furnace, heated seven times hotter than normal, these three men experienced God's presence. And when they finally got out of the furnace, Scripture tells us, they did not even smell of smoke and there was not a burn mark on their bodies or clothes.

It is in that impossible situation that there is no other recourse than an opportunity to see God at work.

I would have loved to talk to these young men following this experience and what it meant to them and how it changed their lives. They experienced God. God was in that furnace and God was on their side, not on the side of the Babylonians.

If we are going to experience the presence of God, we have to be where God can communicate to us. Nebuchadnezzar's fire destroyed the enemy and the bonds holding these three and brought them to a place where they could see God. They enjoyed God's presence. Scripture says they were walking around in a circle. Who in their right mind walks around in the middle of a furnace?

Only those who have experienced God's presence know what this fire did for these three young men. It confirmed to them that God's presence was a reality in their lives.

They never experienced this again, as far as we know. They did not have to. This experience with the presence of God burned a deep impression into their hearts that they would never forget. It was a confirmation of God's presence in their life, no matter what they had to face.

I believe God wants to confirm His presence in my life. I believe when I commit myself totally and completely to God, He will bring me to the place of confirming my relationship with Him.

Imagine somebody walking all their life as a Christian and not having the fiery confirmation that the presence of God is in their midst.

We need to go forward in the power of the Holy Spirit. That power will be the fire of God destroying our enemies and setting us free from all bondage, so that we can walk around joining the son of God in praise and worship unto the Lord.

Old-Time Power

Bring us low in prayer before Thee,
And with faith our souls inspire,
Till we claim, by faith, the promise
Of the Holy Ghost and fire.

—Paul Rader (1879–1938)

CHAPTER 20

The Blessings of God's Manifest Presence

Catch us the foxes, the little foxes that spoil the
vines, for our vines have tender grapes. My beloved
is mine, and I am his. He feeds his flock among
the lilies.

—SONG OF SOLOMON 2:15–16

*Because of Your manifest presence in my life, O Lord, I have
taken great delight in living for You. May my life reflect each
day that presence to the world around me. Amen.*

Throughout this book, I have been talking about coming into the presence of God. I would like to sum it all up in this chapter. What are the blessings that come our way by coming into the fiery presence of God?

My emphasis has been that we need to experience the presence of God. It is not enough just to know about God's presence. Before Moses came to the burning bush, he knew about the presence of God. It was at the burning bush that he experienced God's presence that marked him the rest of his life.

The Bible is very clear in telling us that it is possible to go year after year in spiritual ignorance. We need to understand that what we do not know bankrupts us spiritually.

Understanding and realizing that God's presence is available does not make it so in our lives. The consequence of experiencing God in His fiery presence has a powerful effect on our life. The benefits are beyond our full comprehension.

In thinking about the benefits of daily dwelling in God's presence, the first one I believe would be that it is a deterrent of evil.

The human heart is desperately wicked, and I believe we don't need evidence of that—it is all around us. We as humans are prone to wander. Try to find anything that would deny this. If we are not focused, we are going to be wandering in whatever direction the influence in our life is at the time.

Because this is true, any aid to the disciplinary aspect of our life is welcome. To walk in a life undisciplined is to cause us to wander in the wrong direction. How many have been Christians for twenty-five years and suddenly find themselves far from God? They have wandered. They have been influenced by something other than the manifest presence of God. They truly need a wake-up call.

One thing God's presence creates in our hearts is fear. Fear is a true motive for much of our human conduct. Because of fear we do or don't do certain things. This also has an aspect in our disciplinary walk as a Christian. When we come into the presence of God, a sense of awe and fear comes into our life, which helps provide a deterrent of people in our life.

Most people are run by their habits, allowing outside pressure to guide them daily rather than the fiery presence of God in their life. Because they do not experience God, they have no fear of God.

A thief will not steal in the presence of a policeman. We need to understand that as we come into God's presence, there is going to be that overwhelming fear, a detriment to the evil we have in our life.

The fiery presence of God discourages idleness.

A servant will not loaf around in the presence of his employer. He will want to impress his employer and will want to keep busy doing his job.

When we come into God's presence, we begin to put aside that idleness, and our hearts are stirred up to follow Him.

Plain laziness is a great curse, particularly in the Christian church today. It leaves room for evil. Laziness, as a result of not coming into the presence of God, will cause us not to do the work God wants of us. We know there is vital work to do, but we put it off, and we have reasons for waiting to do it tomorrow.

Laziness weakens and corrupts our soul. We need to have a soul that is on fire with the presence of God, which will push away any idleness that we might have in our lives.

Work does not kill but fretting and maladjustments can. When we think that God is here, we're certainly not in a lull, but we're going to be busy doing our Father's business.

I think the presence of God, this fiery presence, is a cure for carelessness, those little foxes that spoil the Christian vine in the area of our time, our money, our talk, our conduct.

"Thou God sees me . . ."

The carelessness we have in our lives can be dealt with only by experiencing the fiery presence of God and allowing that to be the motivating factor in our lives.

Also, I believe that God's fiery presence in my life is a source of great courage.

If ever the Christian church needed courage, it is today. All the world is against us and we need to be able, with great courage, to stand against the world. We can rest assured in the encouragement that God has for us.

We can also rest assured and secure with a police officer patrolling our door. We don't worry about anything negative happening to us when there are guards out there. A child can whistle in danger because his father is near. So, you see, coming into God's presence creates within me a spirit of courage. I know I'm not alone in this.

When Moses encountered God at that burning bush, he was convinced from that moment on that he wasn't in this alone. Whatever God was calling him to do, he would have the courage to do it because God was with him.

Also, I believe that this fiery presence of God in our life will redeem our labor.

When we understand that God is with us and God is leading and directing us, we will have confidence that God is with us. Our missionaries out in some foreign country are filled with that sense that God is with them. That slum worker trying to redeem some of those people who have gone into a lot of sin and so forth. The martyrs, prisons, all that. We can understand that God is with us. And if God is with us, God is enabling us to do what He wants us to do. And then that labor we are doing is in God's hands. And God is using us and purifying us by the power of His fiery presence for the labor that we are doing for Him.

I must close with this very important aspect. The fire of God's presence in my life will glorify my prayer and worship. The absence of God paralyzes and chills and kills that sense of prayer and worship.

When we are in the presence of God our prayer takes on a vibrancy we cannot know in any other condition. Then our worship begins to be revitalized by His presence. If I'm worshiping in my own strength, it is for naught. When I begin to worship God in the power and demonstration of the Holy Spirit, God's presence so burns in my heart that worship rises above human expectation, entering His holy presence.

The church today needs to have that sense of God's presence taking effect in their prayer and worship life. It's wonderful to know that I'm not on my own when it comes to my prayer life.

Sometimes we get down on our knees and our face before God, and we pray and pray and pray and nothing seems to happen. Nothing seems to go in the direction we would like to see it go. When we begin to experience the fire of God's presence in our life, then our prayers will begin to change.

It is my conviction that most Christians don't know how to pray. But they are not praying as a result of God's presence in their life. Their prayers are just words. But when we experience the fiery presence of God in our lives, our prayers begin to merge with that presence and then we are not praying in our strength anymore, but we are praying in the strength of God's presence in our life.

There is much more I could say about worship here. Sometimes I see in today's churches where worship is certainly not of God. Churches sing and they do this and do that, but there is not a sense of God's presence. Any worship time that does not magnify the presence of God is not acceptable worship to Him.

We can do all we want to do. We can be excited and enthusiastic, but if our worship is not filled with the fire of God's presence, it is not acceptable worship as far as God is concerned.

I tried to make it clear in this book that the presence of God is not something we talk about. It is rather something we experience. When we experience God's presence, our life takes on a dimension that we never had before. And God begins to use us, and the things that we fought before seem to fall away. The things we were trying to chase have disappeared. We begin to have a new focus in our lives and that focus is the fire of God's presence.

How that presence has made a difference in my life is what I rejoice in every day of my life. This is my challenge for you, let us not allow a day to go by without experiencing the fire of God's presence. And then we will see what a difference it makes in our lives.

There's a Song in the Air

There's a song in the air!
There's a star in the sky!
There's a mother's deep prayer
And a baby's low cry!
And the star rains its fire
While the beautiful sing,
For the manger of Bethlehem,
Cradles a King!

—Josiah G. Holland
(1819–1881) /
Karl P. Harrington (1861–1953)

A. W. Tozer (1897–1963) was a self-taught theologian, pastor, and writer whose powerful words continue to grip the intellect and stir the soul of today's believer. He authored more than forty books. *The Pursuit of God* and *The Knowledge of the Holy* are considered modern devotional classics. Get Tozer information and quotes at www.twitter.com/TozerAW.

Reverend James L. Snyder is an award-winning author whose writings have appeared in more than eighty periodicals and fifteen books. He is recognized as an authority on the life and ministry of A. W. Tozer. His first book, *The Life of A. W. Tozer: In Pursuit of God*, won the Reader's Choice Award in 1992 by *Christianity Today*. Because of his thorough knowledge of Tozer, James was given the rights from the A. W. Tozer estate to produce new books derived from over four hundred never-before-published audiotapes. James and his wife live in Ocala, Florida. Learn more at www.jamessnyder ministries.com and www.awtozerclassics.com.

Books by A.W. Tozer

Books by James L. Snyder

More Practical & Inspirational Resources by A.W. Tozer & James L. Snyder

Pulled from A.W. Tozer's sermons, this book captures his teaching on God's will for your life. We all face tough decisions, but Tozer's biblical insight will help guide you on the right path. In the same way that God led His people out of Egypt into the Promised Land, this book will help reveal where God is leading and reassure you that He is by your side.

A Cloud by Day, a Fire by Night

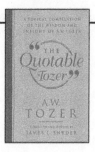

Enjoy the collected wisdom of one of the most beloved Christian authors in history with this seminal guide, ideal for fans, pastors, ministry leaders, and Christian writers. Arranged topically, this quick reference will open your eyes to the depth and insight of Tozer's thoughts on popular culture, the nature of God, spiritual warfare, God's Word, and more.

The Quotable Tozer

This 3-in-1 collection of A.W. Tozer's writings will strengthen your walk with Jesus. *The Pursuit of God* is sure to resonate if you long for a life spent in God's presence. *The Purpose of Man* is a call to worship as God reprioritizes your life and fills your soul. *The Crucified Life* will lead you to the cross so you can be raised to new life in Christ.

The Essential Tozer Collection

You May Also Like . . .

This follow-up to *The Knowledge of the Holy* expounds on Tozer's thoughtful insights and delves deeper into how the attributes of God—the things God has revealed about himself—are a way to understand the Christian life of worship and service.

Delighting in God

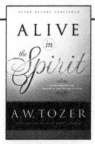

Though every Christian has the Holy Spirit, not every Christian is *filled* with the Spirit. Tozer explains the difference and how, if we use the gifts of the Spirit with wisdom and humility, the evangelical church can become what it was meant to be—and change the world.

Alive in the Spirit

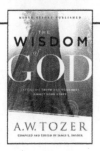

This powerful book captures Tozer's teachings on wisdom as a way to understand the well-lived Christian life. God's wisdom is a part of His character, and knowing this wisdom means drawing closer to Him.

The Wisdom of God

⬥BETHANYHOUSE

You May Also Like ...

BETHANYHOUSE